Assurance of Victory

Assurance of Victory

by
John MacArthur, Jr.

WORD OF GRACE COMMUNICATIONS
P.O. Box 4000
Panorama City, CA 91412

All Scripture quotations, unless noted otherwise, are from the *New
Scofield Reference Bible*, King James Version. Copyright © 1967 by
Oxford University Press, Inc. Reprinted by permission.

Library of Congress Cataloging in Publication Data

MacArthur, John.
  Assurance of victory.

  (John MacArthur's Bible studies)
  Includes index.
  1. Bible.   N.T.   Epistles of John, 1st V—Criticism,
interpretation, etc.   I. Title.   II. Series: MacArthur,
John. Bible studies.
BS2805.2.M32   1986   227'.9406   86-12723
ISBN 0-8024-5130-6 (pbk.)

1 2 3 4 5 6 7 Printing/GB/90 89 88 87 86

Printed in the United States of America

Contents

CHAPTER   PAGE

1. The Victorious Life   7
   Tape GC 2115—1 John 5:1-5

2. The Witness of God   23
   Tape GC 2116—1 John 5:6-12

3. Christian Certainties—Part 1   41
   Tape GC 2117—1 John 5:13-17

4. Christian Certainties—Part 2   59
   Tape GC 2118—1 John 5:17-21

   Scripture Index   77

These Bible studies are taken from messages delivered by Pastor-Teacher John MacArthur, Jr., at Grace Community Church in Panorama City, California. These messages have been combined into a 4-tape album entitled *Assurance of Victory*. You may purchase this series either in an attractive vinyl cassette album or as individual cassettes. To purchase these tapes, request the album *Assurance of Victory* or ask for the tapes by their individual GC numbers. Please consult the current price list; then, send your order, making your check payable to:

WORD OF GRACE COMMUNICATIONS
P.O. Box 4000
Panorama City, CA 91412

Or, call the following toll-free number:
1-800-55-GRACE

1

The Victorious Life

Outline

Introduction
Lesson
I. The Definition of an Overcomer
   A. The Salvation of an Overcomer
      1. An overcomer delineated
      2. An overcomer demonstrated
   B. The Spoils of an Overcomer
      1. Satan
         a) Satan's appearance of victory
            (1) Revelation 6:2
            (2) Revelation 13:7
         b) A Christian's assurance of victory
            (1) Revelation 12:11
            (2) Revelation 15:2
            (3) Revelation 21:7
            (4) Romans 16:20
      2. Death
      3. The world
II. The Description of an Overcomer
   A. Faith in Jesus Christ (vv. 1*a*, 4)
      1. A trust that is total
      2. A faith that is fundamental
   B. Love for Jesus Christ (vv. 1*b*, 5)
      1. Objects of love
      2. Characteristics of love
   C. Obedience to Jesus Christ (vv. 2-3)
      1. Internal obedience
      2. Total obedience
      3. Constant obedience
      4. Cheerful obedience
         a) 2 Corinthians 9:7
         b) Philippians 4:4
III. The Delights of an Overcomer

A. The Tree of Life (Rev. 2:7)
B. Eternal Life (Rev. 2:11)
C. The Bread of Life (Rev. 2:17)
    1. Hidden manna
    2. A white stone
D. The Power of Life (Rev. 2:26-28)
    1. Power over the nations
    2. The morning star
E. The Book of Life (Rev. 3:5)
    1. Clothed in white raiment
    2. Confessed before God
F. The Name of Life (Rev. 3:12)
    1. The "pillar in the temple of my God"
    2. The "name of my God"
G. The Throne of Life (Rev. 3:21)

Introduction

First John 5:1-5 depicts the victorious life. The Bible uses many terms to describe those who have entered into a personal relationship with Jesus Christ. For instance, we are called *Christians*. We are also called "the children of God" (John 1:12), "children of light" (Eph. 5:8), "sons of the day" (1 Thess. 5:5), and "obedient children" (1 Pet. 1:14). But there is another title used in the New Testament, and it is the title *overcomers*. That is the title John uses in 1 John 5:4: "Whatever is born of God overcometh the world; and this is the victory that overcometh the world, even our faith."

Lesson

I. THE DEFINITION OF AN OVERCOMER

A. The Salvation of an Overcomer

Verse 4 tells us that Christians are overcomers. Only those who have been born of God are true overcomers.

1. An overcomer delineated

The Greek word translated *overcomer* literally means "victor." The verb form is *nikaō*, and the noun form is *nik[ma]e*. The verb means "to conquer," "to have victory," "to have superiority." It sometimes means "to defeat."

The Greeks believed that victory could only by achieved by the gods, not by men. Only the gods were conquerors and unconquerable. The Greek goddess of victory was named *Nike*.

2. An overcomer demonstrated

A form of the word *nikaō* is used by our Lord in John 16:33, where He says, "I have overcome the world." It is a word of victory. Jesus, in effect, said, "I have conquered Satan's system." One of the truths about a Christian is that he is in Christ. The Christian is in an indivisible union with Christ Himself and as a result is a partaker of His divine nature. A Christian partakes of everything that Christ is and has, including His inheritance, righteousness, death, life, and Spirit. Since Christ is a victor, Christians partake of His victory. The believer, then, is a victor. Those who have been born of God are true overcomers.

B. The Spoils of an Overcomer

1. Satan

a) Satan's appearance of victory

One of the things Christians have overcome is Satan. We are victors over him. It may seem Satan has victory now, but ultimately he won't.

(1) Revelation 6:2

Revelation 6:2 says, "And I saw and, behold, a white horse; and he [the Antichrist] that sat on him had a bow; and a crown was given unto him, and he went forth conquering, and to conquer." A form of *nikaō* is used here. Satan will have the initial victory. He will cause some devastating things to happen in the early part of the Tribulation as humanity succumbs to him.

(2) Revelation 13:7

Revelation 13:7 says, "It was given unto him to make war with the saints, and to overcome them; and power was given him over all kindreds, and tongues, and nations." Satan will make war with the saints and appear to overcome them. Satan will appear to be the victor.

b) A Christian's assurance of victory

But that isn't the whole story. Ultimately, the book of Revelation says, the saints are going to triumph over Satan.

(1) Revelation 12:11

Revelation 12:11 says, "They overcame him by the blood of the Lamb, and by the word of their testimony; and they loved not their lives unto the death." The saints ultimately will gain the victory.

(2) Revelation 15:2

Revelation 15:2 says, "I saw, as it were, a sea of glass mingled with fire, and them that had gotten the victory over the beast, and over his image, and over his mark, and over the number of his name, standing on the sea of glass, having the harps of God." That is a picture of the victorious saints in heaven, having conquered Satan and his false trinity.

(3) Revelation 21:7

Revelation 21:7 says, "He that overcometh shall inherit all things, and I will be his God, and he shall be my son."

(4) Romans 16:20

Romans 16:20 says, "The God of peace shall bruise Satan under your feet shortly." Satan has been defeated at the cross. The ultimate battle has already been won. Positionally, he is already defeated. But practically—as we learn in the Word of God—we need to exercise that victory on a day-to-day basis.

2. Death

Immediately upon receiving salvation, the Christian overcomes death. First Corinthians 15:54-57 says, "When this corruptible shall have put on incorruption, and this mortal shall have put on immortality, then shall be brought to pass the saying that is written, Death is swallowed up in victory. O death, where is thy sting? O grave, where is thy victory? The sting of death is sin; and the strength of sin is the law. But thanks be to God, who giveth us the victory through our Lord Jesus Christ." The believer conquers death.

3. The world

The third thing a Christian conquers is the world. First John 5:4 says, "Whatever is born of God overcometh the world." The believer is a victor over the invisible, spiritual system of evil that operates in the world to capture men's souls for hell. When someone is saved, he is removed out of the clutches of Satan and hell and reserved for heaven. The believer has conquered the system in Christ. If you look carefully at the phrase "whatever is born of God" in verse 4, you will find it is in the present tense, which means that the Christian is continually having victory over the world. It is a lifelong habit for the saint to conquer the world's system.

What does it mean to be a victor? For one thing, it is foolish to lose when we have the power to overcome. Positionally, we have conquered Satan, death, and the world. But from a practical standpoint, we need to claim and exercise that victory on a day-to-day basis. Christians are overcomers. Everyone else in the world is defeated.

II. THE DESCRIPTION OF AN OVERCOMER

First John 5:1-5 lists three characteristics that are common to all overcomers.

A. Faith in Jesus Christ (vv. 1a, 4)

"Whosoever believeth that Jesus is the Christ is born of God. . . . For whatever is born of God overcometh the world; and this is the victory that overcometh the world, even our faith."

Overcomers are people born of God—people who have put their faith in Jesus Christ. When you place your faith in Christ, you are born of God and become a victor.

1. A trust that is total

We are overcomers by the act of believing, which results in our new birth. All that is required of an overcomer is to believe that Jesus is the anointed One who has come from God. The Greek phrase combines both the present and perfect tense: "Whoever is believing that Jesus is the anointed One has been born of God." If you have been truly born again, you will continue to believe. Some people think all that is required in salvation is a moment of faith. But true Christians have faith from the point of salvation onward. Jesus says in John 8:31, "If ye continue in my word, then are ye my disciples indeed." Sons of God will manifest that they have been begotten of God by continuing to believe in God's eternal, only begotten Son.

2. A faith that is fundamental

First John 5:1 states that a person who is born of God believes that Jesus is the Christ. He must believe that Jesus the man is God incarnate—the Messiah, King, Savior, Redeemer, and the center and focus of revelation. The Cerinthian gnostics, with whom John was dealing, denied that Jesus was the Christ. John said their claims were worthless unless they believed that Jesus is God in human flesh. The Greek word translated "belief" is not referring merely to intellectual attainment or mental acquiescence but a wholehearted acceptance of everything that is implied in the claims of Christ. You need to believe that Jesus is God and that He died for your sins, committing your whole life to Him in sacrifice and serving Him as Lord. That characterizes people who are born of God and are overcomers.

First John 5:4 further defines the concept of faith: "Whatever is born of God overcometh the world; and this is the victory that overcometh the world, even our faith." "Believe" and "faith" are the Greek words *pistas* and *pisteuō*. The essential ingredient in the life of the overcomer is faith. The Christian's victory is based on the reality that Jesus Christ is who He claimed to be.

First John 5:5 says, "Who is he that overcometh the world, but he that believeth that Jesus is the Son of God?" John is emphasizing the need to believe in Christ, because he has already mentioned that phrase many times in the epistle of 1 John and three times in this passage as well. He is saying in verse 5 that the basic characteristic of an overcomer is that he believes in Jesus Christ. A believer's faith overcomes the world.

The Struggle for Solutions

Many people struggle to find solutions for the plagues and problems of life that can't be solved. But Jesus says, "I offer you a life that is victorious over Satan and all his forces, including death and the plagues of the system that corrupt this world. All I ask is that you believe I am God in the flesh who died for your sins and rose again for your justification." If you place your faith in Christ, you are born into a victorious life. I don't want to be victimized by Satan, who goes around as a roaring lion, seeking whom he may devour (1 Pet. 5:8). I don't want to be victimized by death and sent to hell. And I don't want to be victimized by the evil world's system, which tries to take the earth from Christ. If there is victory to be had, I want it. Jesus said you can be a super-conqueror if you believe in Him and are born again. Overcomers are characterized by faith.

B. Love for Jesus Christ (vv. 1*b*, 5)

"And everyone that loveth him that begot loveth him also that is begotten of him. . . . Who is he that overcometh the world, but he that believeth that Jesus is the Son of God?"

It is characteristic of overcomers not only to love God but also to love all who are begotten of God. A true believer confesses Christ and loves his brothers.

1. Objects of love

First John 5:2 says, "By this we know that we love the children of God, when we love God, and keep his commandments." The new birth brings us not only into a relationship with the eternal Son but into a relationship with the children of the Father as well. In 1 John 5:2, John gives a self-evident, universal principle that he has given in many other places (1 John 2:5, 10-11; 3:10; 4:7-8, 12, 21): If you love God, you will love your brothers. Everyone who loves the parent will also love the child. Salvation is not only being in love with God but being in love with God's children as well. If I am born of God, then I will love all who are born of God, for God also dwells in them.

2. Characteristics of love

Love is not a sentiment; it is a sacrificial act. For example, 1 Peter 4:8 says, "Love covers a multitude of sins" (NASB*). If I love someone, I will have a desire to rebuke his sin, cover it, and forgive it. True love doesn't manifest itself by publicizing evil. Love is very practical. That kind of love is characteristic of all who are overcomers, because they love their brothers.

John says the reverse in 1 John 5:2: "By this we know that we love the children of God, when we love God, and keep his commandments." In verse 1 John says that we know we love God because we love our Christian brothers. In verse 2 he says we love them because we love God. Some will say he is reasoning in a circle, and that's exactly right. You can't love the brothers without loving God, and you can't love God without loving the brothers. One proves the other. John is saying it is characteristic of overcomers to love one another.

New American Standard Bible.

13

C. Obedience to Jesus Christ (vv. 2-3)

"By this we know that we love the children of God, when we love God, and keep his commandments. For this is the love of God, that we keep his commandments: and his commandments are not burdensome."

1. Internal obedience

Faith, love, and obedience are all woven together. John ties obedience to love in verse 2: "We love God, and keep his commandments." He ties love to obedience in verse 3: "This is the love of God, that we keep his commandments." And he ties faith to love in verse 1: "Everyone that loveth him that begot loveth him also that is begotten of him." All three are inextricable. Love, faith, and obedience to God's Word are all characteristic of the believer. But the genuine proof of love is obedience.

God wants obedience that is internally—not externally—motivated. God wants us to obey out of love, not fear (1 John 4:18). In Romans 6:17-18 Paul says, "God be thanked, that whereas ye were the servants of sin, ye have obeyed from the heart that form of doctrine which was delivered you. Being, then, made free from sin, ye became the servants of righteousness." Paul was saying the Roman Christians had obeyed from the heart. God doesn't want superficial, external obedience, but obedience that is motivated from the heart.

2. Total obedience

In addition to internal obedience, God wants total obedience. Partial obedience does not satisfy God at all. Some people think God is satisfied when they do a few things right and a few things wrong. But He is not going to settle for two out of three. He wants total obedience. Some people say they believe all the Bible except the part that says wives are to submit to their husbands, but that's not acceptable. In Joshua 22:2-4, Joshua says to the Israelites, "Ye have kept all that Moses, the servant of the Lord, commanded you, and have obeyed my voice in all that I commanded you. Ye have not left your brethren these many days unto this day, but have kept the charge of the commandment of the Lord your God. And now the Lord your God hath given rest unto your brethren, as He promised them." God kept His promise, as their obedience was total and motivated by the heart.

3. Constant obedience

The third kind of obedience that God wants is constant obedience: "Wherefore, my beloved, as ye have always obeyed, not as in my presence only but now much more in my absence, work out your own salvation with fear and trembling" (Phil. 2:12). We're not to be obedient only when we feel like it.

4. Cheerful obedience

The final kind of obedience that God wants is at the heart of what real obedience is: cheerful obedience. Some of you may be wondering how you could possibly obey as God wants you to. But you can.

a) 2 Corinthians 9:7

Paul wrote, "Every man [is to give] according as he purposeth in his heart, so let him give, not grudgingly, or of necessity; for God loveth a cheerful giver." We are commanded to give cheerfully.

b) Philippians 4:4

This verse tells us, "Rejoice in the Lord always; and again I say, Rejoice." Disobedience is a sin, but externally motivated, partial, inconsistent, grudging obedience is also wrong. God wants a loving, total, constant, and joyous response of obedience. He can ask for that because His commandments are not grievous or burdensome (1 John 5:3). Jesus' commandments are not grievous for three reasons: (1) If you fail, He forgives you; (2) He never asks you to do something without giving you the power to do it; and (3) We keep His commandments not out of fear but out of love. That doesn't mean they are never difficult, just that they aren't impossible.

III. THE DELIGHTS OF AN OVERCOMER

John describes the fantastic delights of the overcomer. They are in the book of Revelation. In Revelation 2 and 3 there are seven letters to seven first-century churches. At the end of every letter is a promise to the overcomer. Those promises were given to the true believers in those particular churches, but they also apply to every believer throughout the ages.

A. The Tree of Life (Rev. 2:7)

The first delight of an overcomer is the gift of the tree of life. Revelation 2:7 says, "He that hath an ear, let him hear what the Spirit saith unto the churches: To him that overcometh will I give to eat of the tree of life, which is in the midst of the paradise of God." There was a tree in the Garden of Eden called the tree of the knowledge of good and evil. When Adam and Eve ate of that tree, they became sinners. But there was another tree in the Garden called the tree of life. God took Adam and Eve out of the Garden because He didn't want them to eat from the tree of life; He didn't want sinners to have eternal life because that would have brought sin into His eternal dwelling place. He placed an angel with a flaming sword to guard the Garden so they couldn't get back in and eat from the tree of life.

But did you know that God transplanted that tree out of the Garden into heaven? Revelation 22:2 says, "In the midst of the street of it, and on either side of the river, was there the tree of life, which bore twelve kinds of fruits, and yielded her fruit every month; and the leaves of the tree were for healing of the nations." It's a big tree, since it is on both sides of one river, and it has twelve kinds of fruit. Did you ever see a tree like that? It yields its fruit every month. Its leaves serve as therapy for the nations. The word "healing" doesn't refer to the healing of disease; it refers to providing health. We won't be hungry or thirsty in heaven, but we will eat and drink for pure enjoyment. Revelation 2:7 says, "To him that overcometh will I give to eat of the tree of life, which is in the midst of the paradise of God." That means the overcomer is promised heaven. The first delight for overcomers is the eternal enjoyment of God's presence in His paradise.

B. Eternal Life (Rev. 2:10-11)

The second thing promised to the overcomer is eternal life. Revelation 2:11 says, "He that hath an ear, let him hear what the Spirit saith unto the churches: He that overcometh shall not be hurt of the second death." There are two deaths mentioned in the Bible: the first is physical death, and the second is spiritual death. Spiritual death results in eternal death. The overcomer will not be harmed by the second death. Everyone will die physically. Verse 10 says, "Be thou faithful unto death, and I will give thee a crown of life." The believer will never die spiritually. The man who is not an overcomer dies only to die again. The overcomer dies to live forever.

C. The Bread of Life (Rev. 2:17)

The third delight of an overcomer is the hidden manna of God and a white stone from God. Revelation 2:17 says, "He that hath an ear, let him hear what the Spirit saith unto the churches: To him that overcometh will I give to eat of the hidden manna, and will give him a white stone, and in that stone a new name written, which no man knoweth except he that receiveth it." The overcomer receives two things:

1. Hidden manna

   The first is hidden manna; and that manna is Jesus. People often ask me what heaven will be like. I say, "Heaven is where Jesus is." That's enough for me to know. We will feast on His presence, for Jesus is the hidden manna and the Bread of Life. What a rich banquet, just to spend forever in His presence!

2. A white stone

   God will not only give us manna but a white stone as well. In the Greek text, the white stone refers to a diamond. There is debate about what that might mean. But I have one thought. In the Old Testament, the priest had a bright stone on his breastplate called the Urim. When people wanted to know God's will, He revealed it in that stone. So the white stone may refer to an absolute and ultimate knowledge of God's will. What more could we ask than to have all of God's revelation and knowledge given to us in glory?

   Have you ever thought about what heaven is like? Will we feel like celestial cattle being herded about? No. God is going to give each of us a crystal in which a new name will be written, known only by the person who receives it. My stone will say one thing; yours will say something else. We will all be individuals in glory. What will your new name be? No one will know but you and God.

   We are gong to have a personal relationship with God forever. We're going to be in the presence of the hidden manna—Jesus Christ. We're going to be eating of the tree of life and lapping up the water from the crystal river flowing from His throne. We'll never be touched by the second death. Those are amazing promises.

D. The Power of Life (Rev. 2:26-28)

Revelation 2:26-28 says, "He that overcometh, and keepeth my works unto the end, to him will I give power over the nations; and he shall rule them with a rod of iron; as the vessels of a potter shall they be broken to shivers, even as I received of my Father. And I will give him the morning star."

1. Power over the nations

What is meant by the phrase "power over the nations"? In Psalm 2:8-9 God says He will give power over the nations to the Messiah. Revelation 2:27 says that as Jesus receives power over the nations, He will give it to us. We will rule with Christ in His millenial kingdom.

You may think that Christ will rule harshly since He will rule with a rod. But the Greek word for "rule" is *poimanei* and translated "shepherd." It is a shepherd's rod, not a billy club.

There will be discipline in the kingdom. Where evil and sin dwell, judgment will be enforced. But there will also be care, nourishment, and tenderness in the Shepherd's rod. That is what the phrase "power over the nations" refers to. Could you ever dream of being seated together with Christ on His throne? You may say, "Who me? I'm not even the foreman on my job." But remember, our ruling in the kingdom is by pure grace.

2. The morning star

Revelation 2:28 says, "I will give him the morning star." We own the morning star. Revelation 22:16 says, "I, Jesus, have sent mine angel to testify unto you these things in the churches. I am the root and the offspring of David, and the bright and morning star." Who is the morning star? Jesus. You know who's going to be mine in heaven? Jesus. He is given to overcomers. In 2 Peter 1:19 Peter says, "And the day star [will] arise in your hearts." In a sense, the morning star is already shining in us, but some day He will belong to us in the fullness of His presence. We will rule the nations and possess the Lord of the nations for our very own.

E. The Book of Life (Rev. 3:5)

Revelation 3:5 gives us the fifth delight of an overcomer: "He that overcometh, the same shall be clothed in white raiment; and I will not blot his name out of the book of life, but I will

confess his name before my Father, and before his angels."
Here are two more features of an overcomer:

1. Clothed in white raiment

    The white raiment refers to righteousness, purity, holiness, and glory. We're going to be clothed in white. White is Christ's color. When He comes out of heaven riding on a white horse and wearing a white robe, we will be with him on white horses and dressed in white robes. Because of His own righteousness, He clothes us in His own holiness, purity, and righteousness.

2. Confessed before God

    John further states, "And I will not blot his name out of the book of life, but I will confess his name before my Father, and before His angels" (Rev. 3:5). Many people are confused by that statement. They say, "Does that mean that you could get your name blotted out of the book of life?" No. The text says, "I *will not* blot his name out of the book of life" (emphasis added). We are secure in Christ.

    In John's day, kings had a registry. All the people's names were put into that registry. When anyone committed a criminal act, his name was removed from the registry. Our Lord is saying, "The world may cross you off its list, kings may remove your name for the crime of Christianity, but I will never blot your name out of My book." That doesn't mean you can't be sure; it means you *can* be sure. You are secure in Him. It doesn't imply that God takes names out; it emphasizes that He keeps them in. Aren't you glad that your salvation is guaranteed? He says, "I will confess his name before my Father and before His angels." When I get to heaven, Jesus is going to say, "Father, angels, here is John MacArthur!"

F. The Name of Life (Rev. 3:12)

    Revelation 3:12 says, "Him that overcometh will I make a pillar in the temple of my God, and he shall go no more out; and I will write upon him the name of my God, and the name of the city of my God, the new Jerusalem, which cometh down out of heaven from my God; and I will write upon him my new name."

    1. The "pillar in the temple of my God"

        What does it mean to be a pillar in God's temple? In

19

John's day, an important person was honored by placing a pillar inscribed with his name in the local temple. Great temples to certain gods became monuments of honor to famous citizens because they would mark those pillars with the names of those citizens. As overcomers you and I have pillars in the celestial hall of fame. In fact, we are pillars. We are eternally honored in God's celestial hall of fame.

The verse continues by saying, "And he shall go no more out." Historically, this letter was written to the church at Philadelphia, which was located near a volcano field. They were constantly being subjected to earthquakes. Whenever an earthquake would occur, the people would flee from the city because it was often destroyed. The Lord was saying to this group of believers, "I'm going to make you pillars, and you're never going to have to flee. You're never going to have to fear. In heaven there is no fear. No pillar has ever collapsed there. You're secure."

2. The "name of my God"

    In addition, Jesus is going to write on us "the name of my God," which is the mark of possession. Then He is going to write "the name of the city of my God, the new Jerusalem, which cometh down out of heaven from my God." That is the mark of citizenship. Then He will write "my new name," which is the mark of love. We belong to God, to heaven, and to Jesus. We'll be pillars, never shaken, never fearful, never having to run.

G. The Throne of Life (Rev. 3:21)

    The seventh delight of an overcomer is mentioned in Revelation 3:21: "To him that overcometh will I grant to sit with me in my throne, even as I also overcame, and am set down with my Father in his throne." The supreme thing is to be in heaven seated on the throne of God. We will be co-reigning with Jesus, sitting in His throne, and He will be sitting in the Father's throne. We are all going to be in the same place.

    Do you have a picture of what it means to be an overcomer and to someday enjoy the delights of being an overcomer forever? I praise God that I am an overcomer.

Focusing on the Facts

1. Who are the only true overcomers according to 1 John 5:4 (see p. 2)?
2. What are the various renderings of the word *overcomer* (see p. 2)?
3. What are the three major things Christians have victory over (see pp. 3-5)?
4. What three things must characterize all who are considered true overcomers (see pp. 5-8)?
5. The essential ingredient in the life of the overcomer is his _____ (see p. 6).
6. What self-evident, universal principle does the apostle John give in 1 John 5:2 (see p. 7)?
7. What is the genuine proof of love (see pp. 7-8)?
8. List the four kinds of obedience God desires from us (see pp. 8-9).
9. Out of that list, which of the four is at the heart of real obedience (see p. 9)?
10. There are three reasons Jesus' commands are not burdensome. What are they (see p. 9)?
11. What are the seven delights of an overcomer (see pp. 9-14)?
12. Why did God expel man from the Garden of Eden (see p. 10)?
13. What is the result of receiving the gift of the tree of life (see p. 10)?
14. What are the two deaths described in the Bible and what is the result of both (see pp. 10-11)?
15. What is the meaning of the hidden manna and the white stone (see p. 11)?
16. What is meant by the phrase "power over the nations" (see p. 12)?
17. Who is the "morning star" (see p. 12)?
18. Explain two features associated with being in the book of life (see pp. 12-13).
19. What does it mean to be a "pillar in the temple of my God" (see pp. 13-14)?
20. What distinctive marks were mentioned in the sixth delight, the "name of life" (see p. 14)?
21. What is the supreme delight of an overcomer (see p. 14)?

Pondering the Principles

1. Throughout the centuries, athletes have endured grueling training to gain victory and the spoils that come with it, only to find that victory is often elusive. Christians, however, as overcomers, have complete certainty about the ultimate victory, which is eternal life with Jesus Christ (see 1 John 5:11-13). Look up the following Scripture verses and write out how you can have

victory over Satan (Matt. 4:1-11), death (John 5:24; Rom. 6:3-9), and the world (1 John 5:4; John 17:14). 2. It was said that faith, love, and obedience are inextricably linked, and that the genuine proof of love is obedience through faith (see pp. 5-9).

2. Take a pen or pencil and draw a triangle with each of those words at the points, writing obedience at the top. Now look up the following verses that deal with those three areas, and try to match them with the right word: Hebrews 11:1; 2 Corinthians 10:5; John 13:34; 1 Peter 1:22; 2 Corinthians 5:7; Romans 12:9. Think of other verses dealing with those areas, write them beside the correct word, and memorize them.

3. In Revelation 2 and 3, we read about seven delights of an overcomer (see pp. 9-14). Take one of the seven each day, write it out, and pray, thanking God that you are an overcomer. Think of specific things throughout the day that remind you of those rewards. Continue to thank God that you are an overcomer.

2
The Witness of God

Outline

Introduction
A. The Preparation for the Witness
  1. In John's epistle
  2. In John's gospel
B. The Pattern of the Witness
  1. The grammatical pattern
  2. The historical pattern
  3. The numerical pattern
    a) Deuteronomy 19:15
    b) Matthew 18:19-20
    c) 2 Corinthians 13:1
    d) Hebrews 11:1-2; 12:1
C. The Purpose of the Witness
  1. John 1:15
  2. John 5:32, 36
  3. John 8:13-18
Lesson
I. The External Witness (vv. 6-9)
  A. The Contemporary Denial
    1. Recounting the gnostic heresy
    2. Refuting the gnostic heresy
    3. Reaffirming the Spirit's witness
  B. The Corroborating Data
    1. The witness of the water
      a) The baptism of Jesus (Matt. 3:13-16)
      b) The baptism of the Holy Spirit (Matt. 3:11-12)
      c) The mark of the Holy Spirit (Matt. 3:17)
      d) The guidance of the Holy Spirit (John 1:32)
    2. The witness of the blood
      a) The Roman soldier's confession
      b) The Holy Spirit's cooperation
      c) The Father's confirmation
      d) The thief and the centurion's confirmation

      e) The prophetic confirmation
   3. The witness of the Spirit
      a) The Spirit's record
      b) The Pharisees' response
         (1) Their conclusion was absurd (Matt. 12:22-26)
         (2) The truth was obscured (Matt. 12:28)
         (3) Their evil was exposed (Matt. 12:31-32, 34)
II. The Internal Witness (vv. 10-12)
  A. The Believer's Confidence (v. 10*a*)
    1. Expressed in Romans 8:15-16
    2. Expressed in Galatians 4:6
  B. The Unbeliever's Choice (vv. 10*b*-12)
    1. Reject the evidence (v. 10*b*)
    2. Receive the evidence (vv. 11-12)

Introduction

First John 5:6-12 speaks about the witness of God: "This is he that came by water and blood, even Jesus Christ; not by water only, but by water and blood. And it is the Spirit that beareth witness, because the Spirit is truth. . . . And there are three that bear witness in earth, the Spirit, and the water, and the blood; and these three agree in one. If we receive the witness of men, the witness of God is greater; for this is the witness of God which he hath testified of his Son. He that believeth on the Son of God hath the witness in himself; he that believeth not God hath made him a liar, because he believeth not the record that God gave of his Son. And this is the record, that God hath given to us eternal life, and this life is in his Son. He that hath the Son hath life; and he that hath not the Son of God hath not life."

The theme of this passage is the term "witness." The word "record" in some translations is identical to the word "witness." Verse 9 says, "If we receive the witness of men, the witness of God is greater; for this is the witness of God which he hath testified of his Son." God is involved in attesting to a great truth: the deity of our Lord Jesus Christ. If someone is a true witness of God, he will manifest the pattern of this passage.

  A. The Preparation for the Witness

    1. In John's epistle

       First John 5:4-5 says, "Whatever is born of God overcometh the world; and this is the victory that overcometh the world, even our faith. Who is he that overcometh the world, but he that believeth that Jesus is the Son of God?" Jesus Christ is God in human flesh, who took upon Himself the form of a Son in servitude. To be an overcomer is to believe that Jesus is who He said He was, and the key to that is faith.

To have faith in something, you have to be convinced that object is worthy of your faith. I'm not going to drive my car across a bridge unless I think it's going to hold me up. Likewise, I'm not going to put my faith in the Lord Jesus Christ unless there is some evidence that He is worthy of my faith. Having stated that we need to believe in Jesus Christ, John tells us why we should in 1 John 5:6. He gives us the testimony of God about who Jesus is and gives us a warning in verse 10: "He that believeth not God hath made him a liar, because he believeth not the record that God gave of his Son."

2. In John's gospel

Throughout his gospel, John states our need to believe in Jesus Christ. John 20:31 says, "These are written, that ye might believe that Jesus is the Christ, the Son of God; and that believing ye might have life through his name." The entire gospel is filled with evidence that Jesus is God by the clear witness of the Father. Jesus said repeatedly, "The Father who sent me has himself testified concerning me" (John 5:37, NIV*; cf. John 8:18) and, "He [the Father] will bear witness of Me" (John 15:26, NASB). The gospel of John was written as irrefutable evidence that Jesus is God and that in believing you might have eternal life. John is saying the same thing in 1 John 5:4. We believe because we see and hear the witness of God and are convinced it is true.

B. The Pattern of the Witness

The word "witness" deserves study because it is used nine times in this text alone and is therefore the key to this passage.

1. The grammatical pattern

The word "witness" appears 168 times in the New Testament. The Greek word is *martureō*, from which we get the English word "martyr." The noun form is *marturia*. The root word means, "One who remembers or who has knowledge of something by personal experience." In biblical and extrabiblical literature, it has been

---

*New International Version.

used of a witness to facts in a legal matter. For example, that term appears in the trial of Christ. It can be used to describe those who witness or give testimony to truth of any kind.

2. The historical pattern

    The word "witness" was used in the Septuagint, the Greek translation of the Old Testament. Isaiah 43:9 says, "Let all the nations be gathered together, and let the people be assembled. Who among them can declare this, and show us former things? Let them bring forth their witnesses, that they may be justified; or let them hear, and say, It is truth." Here God is calling together all the nations in a trial-like setting to decide whose God is real, which is reminiscent of Elijah on Mount Carmel (1 Kings 18:20-40). The nations are given the opportunity to witness about the deity of their gods.

    The scene continues in Isaiah 44:9-11: "They that make a carved image are all of them vanity; and their delectable things shall not profit; and they are their own witnesses; they see not, nor know, that they may be ashamed." God is saying the idol itself attests to the fact that it is man-made and therefore without knowledge or speech. He says further in verses 10-11: "Who hath formed a god, or melted and cast an image that is profitable for nothing? Behold, all his fellows shall be ashamed; and the workmen, they are of men. Let them all be gathered together, let them stand up; yet they shall fear, and they shall be ashamed together." All nations are brought in who worship idols, and it is agreed by their testimony that their gods are absolutely useless.

    In Isaiah 43:10-12 God speaks to Israel and says, "Ye are my witnesses, saith the Lord, and my servant whom I have chosen, that ye may know and believe me, and understand that I am he; before me there was no God formed, neither shall there be after me. I, even I, am the Lord, and beside me there is no savior. I have declared, and have saved, and I have shown, when there was no strange god among you; therefore, ye are my witnesses, saith the Lord, that I am God." Isaiah 44:8 says, "Fear not, neither be afraid; have not I told thee from that time, and have declared it? Ye are even my witnesses. Is there a God beside me? Yea, there is no God; I know not any." If God doesn't know of any other gods, then there aren't any. Three times God referred to Israel as His witnesses. They were to relay to men the truth that He is God and give testimony to the existence and character of God. All 168 uses of the root word *martus* give evidence that something is true. According to 1 John 5:6-12, then, God is giving witness to the truth of the deity of Jesus Christ.

3. The numerical pattern

Another feature about witnesses in the Bible is that one witness isn't sufficient. The one witness might be truthful, but to convince men of the truth, the Bible prescribes at least two or three witnesses.

a) Deuteronomy 19:15—"One witness shall not rise up against man for any iniquity, or for any sin, in any sin that he sinneth; at the mouth of two witnesses, or at the mouth of three witnesses, shall the matter be established." There is an obvious reason for more than one witness. It would be too easy for false accusations to occur if you didn't have at least two or three witnesses.

b) Matthew 18:19-20—"Again I say unto you that if two of you shall agree on earth as touching any thing that they shall ask, it shall be done for them by my Father, who is in heaven. For where two or three are gathered together in my name, there am I in the midst of them." The Scriptures declare that there should be two or three witnesses in all cases. In our day, that is also standard procedure.

c) 2 Corinthians 13:1—The apostle Paul said, "This is the third time I am coming to you. In the mouth of two or three witnesses shall every word be established." God always gives testimony to Himself and to His Son through multiple testimony.

d) Hebrews 11:1-2; 12:1—"Faith is the substance of things hoped for, the evidence of things not seen. For by it the elders received witness." The elders received God's witness concerning faith and lived lives that passed on that witness. Chapter 12 begins, "Seeing we . . . are compassed about with so great a cloud of witnesses, let us lay aside every weight, and the sin which doth so easily beset us, and let us run with patience the race that is set before us." The elders received the witness in chapter 11 and spread it throughout their ministry. Now they stand as a great cloud of witnesses.

God's formula is simple: Reveal the truth to men who in turn pass it on to others. He revealed His witness to the apostles, who wrote the New Testament and passed it on to us. We in turn receive the truth from the apostles and pass it on as God's continuing witnesses.

C. The Purpose of the Witness

There is much material in the New Testament that witnesses to the deity of Christ. John's primary concern, as is the concern of every New Testament writer, is that this witness leads to the conviction that Jesus is God. They were not trying to say He was a miracle worker or a man who was able to tune in with God, able to tap into divine power. The Bible portrays Christ as God in human flesh. The ultimate witness is not what He did but who He is. Many say, "Oh, yes, Jesus is a wonderful person. Just look at what He did." That isn't the entire point. You need to move from the interpretation of what He did to who He is.

1. John 1:15—"John [the Baptist] bore witness of [Christ], and cried, saying, This was he of whom I spoke, He that cometh after me is preferred before me; for he was before me." The one John had spoken of was the coming Messiah.

2. John 5:32, 36—Jesus said, "There is another that beareth witness of me; and I know that the witness which he witnesseth of me is true" (v. 32). He continued in verse 36: "I have greater witness than that of John; for the works which the Father hath given me to finish, the same works that I do, bear witness of me, that the Father hath sent me." Jesus was saying, "I want you to see who I am by what I've done."

3. John 8:13-18—"The Pharisees, therefore, said unto him, Thou bearest witness of thyself; thy witness is not true. Jesus answered, and said unto them, Though I bear witness of myself, yet my witness is true; for I know from where I came, and where I go; but ye cannot tell from where I come, and where I go. Ye judge after the flesh; I judge no man. And yet if I judge, my judgment is true; for I am not alone, but I and the Father that sent me. It is also written in your law, that the testimony of two men is true. I am one that bear witness of myself, and the Father

that sent me beareth witness of me." Throughout John's gospel, God bears witness about who Christ is.

Lesson

God is the great witness to the Son of God. He has witnessed throughout history to the truth of the Messiah. In 1 John 5:6-12, John presents two kinds of testimony: external and internal.

I. THE EXTERNAL WITNESS (vv. 6-9)

A. The Contemporary Denial

First John 5:6 says, "This is he that came by water and blood, even Jesus Christ; not by water only, but by water and blood. And it is the Spirit that beareth witness, because the Spirit is truth." God has given witness to Christ in a very objective and historical way. But Christ's contemporaries weren't convinced that He was the Son of God. They said He was a liar, deceiver, drunkard, rebel, fanatic, and madman. Some would even say that because His contemporaries didn't believe in Him, He is not believable today. Evidence is needed to believe in Christ. There are three witnesses listed in verse 6 establishing that Jesus is God incarnate: the water, the blood, and the Spirit. The water and blood in this verse can refer to only two things: Christ's baptism and death. God has given testimony to the deity of Jesus by Christ's baptism and death.

1. Recounting the gnostic heresy

John adds, "Not by water only, but by water and blood" (v. 6). The gnostics taught that Jesus was only a man. They believed all matter and flesh was evil but that spirit was good. Since God is spirit (John 4:24), they assumed He would never become a man and pollute Himself; thus they concluded Jesus was only a man. They believed that at the baptism of Jesus, the Christ spirit—the dove—rested on Jesus, and that He then became the spokesman for God's truth. They also taught that, prior to the cross, the divine Christ left again because they assumed divinity would never suffer crucifixion.

2. Refuting the gnostic heresy

John renounced the gnostic heresy by reaffirming that Jesus was the Messiah from His baptism through His death. His baptism was a part of His messiahship, and so was His death. Any heresy that denies the efficacy of

Jesus' death and blood for the sins of the world is satanic. John affirms that Jesus Christ was the man Jesus and the Christ of God from His birth to His death—and forever. Some day you will see Jesus with nail prints on His hands and feet in a glorified body, but He will be no less God. You will not see God the Father, for He is spirit. From His incarnation and throughout all eternity, Jesus will maintain that duality. Cerinthus and his gnostic friends are dead, and their creed is dead with them, but today many other heresies deny the deity of Christ. If Jesus hadn't died on the cross as a man, He could not have paid for the sins of men, and if He weren't God, His death wouldn't have meant anything because He would not have had the power to overcome sin. The resurrection is evidence that Jesus is the Messiah.

3. Reaffirming the Spirit's witness

Verse 6 says, "It is the Spirit that beareth witness, because the Spirit is truth." John is speaking of the testimony of God that comes through the Holy Spirit. You can believe what the Holy Spirit says because He is truth. Jesus said, "I am the way, the truth, and the life" (John 14:6). The Bible says that God is a God of truth (Ps. 31:5), and the Holy Spirit is called the Spirit of truth (John 14:17), so They all speak truth. The Holy Spirit continuously bears the supreme witness to the world about the deity of Jesus Christ.

B. The Corroborating Data

Three witnesses corroborate Christ's deity.

1. The witness of the water

a) The Baptism of Jesus (Matt. 3:13-16)

Matthew 3:13 says, "Then cometh Jesus from Galilee to the Jordan unto John [the Baptist], to be baptized by him." John the Baptist was the last Old Testament-type prophet. He administered a Jewish ceremonial cleansing for repentance. He baptized as a sign of inward cleansing to prepare the people for the coming of Messiah.

Jesus, the true Messiah, arrived to be baptized by John. Verse 14 says, "But John forbade Him, saying, I have need to be baptized of thee, and comest thou to me?" John was saying, "I'm the sinner. I should be baptized by You!" He believed the lesser could be blessed only by the greater. "And Jesus answering said unto him, Permit it to be so now; for thus it becometh us to fulfill all righteousness" (v. 15). Jesus was saying, "I have to fulfill all God's requirements." And in every sense, Jesus identified with and honored God's laws and standards. For example, when it came time to pay the Temple tax, Jesus paid it. When it was time for Jesus to fulfill God's standard for repentance and ceremonial washing, He honored it by identifying Himself with the messianic people and their sin. It was God's will that all Israel be baptized and prepared for the kingdom, thus God's own Son claimed no exemption to God's standards. He set the perfect example of obedience to every area of God's standard.

Matthew 3:16 says, "Jesus, when he was baptized, went up straightway out of the water; and, lo, the heavens were opened unto him, and he saw the Spirit of God descending like a dove, and lighting upon him." The text says that the Spirit descended *"like* a dove" (emphasis added). Some people think it was a dove. I think it might have been the appearance of light in the form of a dove.

b) The baptism of the Holy Spirit (Matt. 3:11-12)

That kind of appearance by the Spirit must have shocked John the Baptist because he was in the tradition of the Old Testament prophets. Very often in the Old Testament when the Spirit of God came on the body, there was a violent shaking. But this time, all was calm and peaceful. In Matthew 3:11-12, John the Baptist is preaching about the Messiah: "I, indeed, baptize you with water unto repentance, but he who cometh after me is mightier than I, whose shoes I am not worthy to bear; he shall baptize you with the Holy Spirit, and with fire; whose fan is in his hand, and he will thoroughly purge his floor, and gather his wheat into the granary, but he will burn up the chaff with unquenchable fire." John conceived of fierce judgment when the Messiah came, but when Jesus arrived, the Holy Spirit appeared as a dove, not as fire. The baptism of the Holy Spirit with fire refers to the Judgment Day. Some people want to make this passage refer to the Day of Pentecost, but that wouldn't be correct because the people at Pentecost did not burn up with unquenchable fire. The first time Jesus came, He came in meekness and lowliness, riding on a donkey. But the next time He comes, He will be King of kings and Lord of lords.

c) The mark of the Holy Spirit (Matt. 3:17)

Many people think that before this time Jesus did not possess the Holy Spirit, but that cannot be true because He is God and therefore has always possessed the Holy Spirit. The baptism of Christ was God's way of putting His stamp of approval on the public ministry of Jesus Christ. Matthew 3:17 says, "And, lo, a voice from heaven, saying, This is my beloved Son, in whom I am well pleased." God's testimony came right out of heaven proclaiming Jesus as the Son of God. Christ's baptism marked the beginning of His special ministry.

d) The guidance of the Holy Spirit (John 1:32)

The Holy Spirit was a constant guide to the earthly ministry of Jesus Christ. The entire Trinity is seen in operation in His ministry. The Father's approval is seen in Matthew 3:17, and the Spirit's role is seen in John 1:32: "And John [the Baptist] bore witness, saying, I saw the Spirit descending from heaven like a dove, and it abode [rested] upon him." The Holy Spirit remained fixed on Christ and controlled His human nature. When Jesus—God in human flesh—came into the world, He did not cease to be God but restricted the use of His divine powers to what the Holy Spirit wanted to accomplish. He simply became a Son, a servant through whom the Holy Spirit worked. Jesus restricted the use of His divine powers and became a living illustration of obedience through which the Holy Spirit took control.

2. The witness of the blood

The second testimony was given at the cross.

a) The Roman soldier's confession

First John 5:6 says, "This is he that came by water and blood, even Jesus Christ; not by water only, but by water and blood." There was an unbelieving Roman soldier at the cross when Christ died, but in Matthew

27:54 he says, "Truly, this was the Son of God." The cross witnessed to the deity of Jesus Christ.

b)   The Holy Spirit's cooperation

The Holy Spirit was also involved in giving testimony to the deity of Christ at the cross. Hebrews 9:14 says, "How much more shall the blood of Christ, who through the eternal Spirit offered himself without spot to God, purge your conscience from dead works to serve the living God?" Christ, by restricting His divine prerogatives, set the pattern for a life of service and obedience. We also are to restrict our own desires and let the Holy Spirit order our lives.

c)   The Father's confirmation

There was also a staggering amount of confirmation by God the Father at the cross. The first thing He did was cause complete darkness to occur in the middle of the day. There were earthquakes and opened tombs and people raised from the dead after the resurrection. The veil in the Temple was ripped from top to bottom.

d)   The thief and the centurion's confirmation

The thief on the cross recognizes God the Father's witness and says in Luke 23:41: "And we, indeed, [suffer] justly; for we receive the due reward of our deeds. But this man [Christ] hath done nothing amiss." The thief was redeemed that day while a Roman centurion stood by and affirmed God's witness (Matt. 27:54).

e)   The prophetic confirmation

So many prophecies were fulfilled at the cross that it's hard to think of them all. John 19:18 tells us that they crucified Christ and fulfilled the story of the brazen serpent given in Numbers 21. Psalm 22 gives so many prophetic details of the Messiah's death that any Jewish person who knew Psalm 22 and stood at the cross would have realized that all those prophecies were being fulfilled. Psalm 22:14-16 says, "I am poured out like water, and all my bones are out of joint: my heart is like wax; it is melted within me. My strength is dried up like a potsherd, and my tongue cleaveth to my jaws; and thou hast brought me into the dust of death. For dogs have compassed me; the assembly of the wicked have enclosed me; they pierced my hands and my feet."

That prophecy gives witness to the Promised One, the Messiah. Verse 18 says, "They part my garments among them, and cast lots upon my vesture." Verse 24 says, "He hath not despised nor abhorred the affliction of the afflicted, neither hath he hidden his face from him; but when he cried unto him, he heard." That is a marvelous fulfillment of the exaltation of Christ by the Father (cf. Phil. 2:8-11).

Isaiah 53:2 says of the Messiah, "There is no beauty that we should desire him." He wasn't handsome but was "brought as a lamb to the slaughter" (v. 7). Every prophecy concerning the Messiah's death was fulfilled to the very letter at the cross. The New Testament records for us about 332 prophecies fulfilled concerning Christ. Many of them were fulfilled at the cross. In John 19:30 Jesus says, "It is finished." He was God right to the finish. Throughout Christ's crucifixion, the Holy Spirit witnessed to His deity. If you look at the cross of Christ, study the facts, and do not believe Jesus is the Son of God, your problem isn't a lack of confirming witnesses; your problem is sin. The evidence is irrefutable.

3. The witness of the Spirit

The apostle John says there's a third witness to Christ's deity: the Holy Spirit. His witness is twofold. First, it's objective—historical and external. And second, it is subjective—personal and internal.

a) The Spirit's record

The Holy Spirit's witness to the deity of Christ is presented throughout Scripture. In Luke 1:35 the Bible says that Christ was conceived by the Holy Spirit. Mark 1:12 says Christ was led by the Spirit, Acts 10:38 says He was empowered by the Spirit, and Luke 4:14, 18-19 says He was filled with the Spirit. All through Christ's life the Spirit was at work giving testimony to who He was.

b) The Pharisees' response

(1) Their conclusion was absurd (Matt. 12:22-26)

Matthew 12:22-24 says, "Then was brought unto him one possessed with a demon, blind, and dumb; and he [Jesus] healed him, insomuch that the blind and dumb both spoke and saw. And all the people were amazed, and said, Is not this the son of David? But when the Pharisees heard it, they said, This fellow doth not cast out demons, but by Beelzebub, the prince of the demons." The Pharisees' response to Christ should have been that He was the Messiah, but their response to His healing of the demoniac was the exact opposite. They said He cast the demon out by Satan's power and was therefore satanic. The Pharisees' conclusion was absurd. Verses 25-26 say, "Jesus knew their thoughts, and said unto them, Every kingdom divided against itself is brought to desolation; and every city or house divided against itself shall not stand. And if Satan cast out Satan, he is divided against himself; how shall then his kingdom stand?" Satan does not go about casting out Satan.

(2) The truth was obscured (Matt. 12:28)

The second thing the Pharisees did was to obscure the truth. In Matthew 12:28 Jesus says, "But if I cast out demons by the Spirit of God, then the kingdom of God is come unto you." Jesus was saying that if they believed their lie, they were going to miss the kingdom and obscure the truth in the meantime.

(3) Their evil was exposed (Matt. 12:31-32, 34)

Verse 34 says, "O generation of vipers [snakes], how can ye, being evil, speak good things? For out of the abundance of the heart the mouth speaketh." Jesus' response was: "What you do, you do by Satan." Verses 31-32 are the key to the passage: "Wherefore, I say unto you, All manner of sin and blasphemy shall be forgiven men; but the blasphemy against the Holy Spirit shall not be forgiven men. And whosoever speaketh a word against the Son of man, it shall be forgiven him; but whosoever speaketh against the Holy Spirit, it shall not be forgiven him, neither in this age, neither in the age to come." That passage refers to the unpardonable sin. Their conclusion was to attribute the works of the Spirit to Satan, and that is unpardonable. The works of the Spirit were to convince men that Christ is God. But the Pharisees were 180 degrees from the truth and were hopelessly lost.

Throughout 1 John, God has been saying that Jesus is God in human flesh. Based on that witness, we are to believe what He says. According to 1 John 5:6-9, we are to believe because of the multitude of witnesses: the water, the blood, and the Spirit. The Holy Spirit was active at the baptism of Jesus, at the cross, and in the miracles He produced in Christ's life. That's all one great testimony.

First John 5:9 is a transition verse to the second main point: the internal witness. It says, "If we receive the witness of men, the witness of God is greater; for this is the witness of God which he hath testified of his Son." God was giving testimony at Christ's baptism, the cross, and through the Spirit. It is God who bore witness in the external water and the blood, and it is God also who gives the internal witness.

II. THE INTERNAL WITNESS (vv. 10-12)

A. The Believer's Confidence (v. 10a)

"He that believeth on the Son of God hath the witness in himself."

We not only have the witness of God in the record of Scripture and history, but if you believe in the Son of God, that witness is confirmed in your heart as well. One of the reasons I know I'm a Christian is that I know it for a fact in my heart. The Bible teaches that there is an internal, subjective testimony of the Holy Spirit.

1. Expressed in Romans 8:15-16

   Romans 8:15-16 says, "Ye have not received the spirit of bondage again to fear; but ye have received the Spirit of adoption, whereby we cry, Abba, Father. The Spirit himself beareth witness with our spirit, that we are the children of God." When we believe in Christ, God bears witness within us by His Spirit that we are true children of God. That is something an unbeliever will never experience.

2. Expressed in Galatians 4:6

Galatians 4:6 says, "Because ye are sons, God hath sent forth the Spirit of His Son into your hearts, crying, Abba, Father." The Spirit gives us confidence that we are children of God, and we respond by calling the Father "Abba," which means "Papa" or "Daddy." The Spirit witnesses not only externally in history but also internally when you believe. Some might say, "I see the external evidence, but I'm not too sure about this internal witness." If you believe and take the step of faith, the witness will be confirmed in your heart by the presence of the Holy Spirit.

B. The Unbeliever's Choice (vv. 10b-12)

There are only two possible responses to the testimony of God:

1. Reject the evidence (v. 10b)

"He that believeth not God hath made him a liar, because he believeth not the record that God gave of his Son."

If a man refuses to accept the witness of God regarding Christ in Scripture and the evidence of what He has done through the Holy Spirit, he is standing defiantly before God and calling Him a liar. Continued unbelief is not just a misfortune to be pitied but a sin to be hated. It is the one thing for which man will never be forgiven, because it contradicts the Word of God and calls God a liar. There is no place for being patronizing or sympathetic with people who reject God's clear testimony. They are not to be treated as poor misguided souls but as blatant blasphemers. A man is a fool who waves his frail fist in the face of Almighty God and calls Him a liar. That is exactly what happens when someone denies that Christ is God incarnate. Judgment is the fate of those who reject the clear and true testimony of God, for God is not a liar (Titus 1:2; Heb. 6:18; Num. 23:19).

2. Receive the evidence (vv. 11-12)

"This is the record, that God hath given to us eternal life, and this life is in his Son. He that hath the Son hath life; and he that hath not the Son of God hath not life."

Because you accept God's witness, His gift to you is eternal life. John now forgets the rejecting unbeliever and speaks to the believer, one who receives the witness of

God. God has given clear, irrefutable testimony. Every man has the opportunity to act as a judge and draw a verdict. If he chooses to reject the witness concerning Christ, he stands with fist clenched, calling God a liar; but if he responds to the witness of God, he receives eternal life.

What Is Eternal Life?

1. Eternal life is the divine presence of Jesus in us

    First John 5:20 says, "We know that the Son of God is come, and hath given us an understanding, that we may know him that is true; and we are in him that is true, even in his Son Jesus Christ. This is the true God, and eternal life." To receive eternal life is to receive the divine presence of Jesus Christ.

2. Eternal life is a gift

    First John 5:11 says, "This is the record, that God hath given to us eternal life, and this life is in his Son." Eternal life is a gift to us given by the Son of God.

3. Eternal life is a present and forever possession

    The moment you believe in Christ, you receive the gift of eternal life, and it will be yours throughout all eternity.

    The last thing Jesus said before He ascended to the Father was, "Ye shall receive power, after the Holy Spirit is come upon you; and ye shall be witnesses unto me both in Jerusalem, and in all Judaea, and in Samaria, and unto the uttermost part of the earth" (Acts 1:8). The question you need to ask yourself is, "Am I a true witness of God?"

Focusing on the Facts

1. What word characterizes the theme of 1 John 5:6-12 (see p. 18)?
2. What great truth is God attesting to in this passage (see p. 18)?
3. What is the key to being an overcomer (see p. 19)?
4. What does the apostle John state as his reason for writing his gospel (John 20:31; see p. 19)?
5. What is the key word to 1 John 5:6-12 (see p. 19)?
6. What does the root word for "witness" literally mean (see p. 19)?
7. Why is one witness not sufficient according to the Bible (see p. 21)?
8. What is God's formula in revealing His witness to man (see p. 22)?
9. What was the main concern of every New Testament writer (see p. 22)?

10. True or false: The ultimate witness to Christ is what He did, not who He is (see p. 22).
11. Who did Christ's contemporaries think He was (see p. 23)?
12. There are three witnesses in 1 John 5:6 that give testimony to the deity of Jesus Christ. What are they (see pp. 24-28)?
13. Explain the witness of the blood—the many things that were going on during the death of Christ (see pp. 26-28).
14. What is the source of any heresy that denies the efficacy of the death and resurrection of Christ (see pp. 23-24)?
15. Explain why it is important that Jesus be both man and God (see p. 24).
16. Why did Jesus insist that He be baptized by John the Baptist (see pp. 24-25)?
17. Why might John the Baptist have been surprised at the coming of the Messiah (see p. 25)?
18. What was the reason for the Holy Spirit's descending as a dove on Jesus (see pp. 25-26)?
19. What were five specific things going on during the death of Christ (see pp. 26-28)?
20. What would a Jewish person have to conclude after seeing the crucifixion (see p. 27)?
21. What is the twofold witness of the Holy Spirit concerning the deity of Christ (see p. 28)?
22. How did the Pharisees respond to the deity of Christ (see pp. 28-29)?
23. What is the meaning of the unpardonable sin mentioned in Matthew 12 (see pp. 28-29)?
24. Cite two Scripture passages that clearly teach about the internal witness of the Holy Spirit (see pp. 30-31).
25. What are the two ways to respond to Christ's deity? Explain the result of both (see pp. 31-32).

Pondering the Principles

1. Do you have any unsaved friends who need to be convinced of the deity of Jesus Christ? Think of how God has witnessed to you internally through the Spirit and externally through Christ's death. How do you think you could witness to them concerning those truths? What changes in your life must you make to be a better witness? Ask God right now to begin to change you to be that better witness. Ask Him for specific opportunities to begin to share the truths you've learned in this chapter with those whom you know desperately need them.

2. Why is it that so many people deny the deity of our Lord Jesus

Christ? Is it because of a lack of convincing evidence or because of a deliberate refusal of the facts? Write down all the reasons you can think of explaining why so many deny the witness of God. Take that list and look again at the verses in this chapter that confirm the deity of Christ. Answer the critics' claims, just as Jesus did the Pharisees' in Matthew 12:22-32.

3. Many people are unsure of their salvation, even those who have grown up in churches and Christian homes. Part of the Holy Spirit's job is to internally confirm the validity of a person's salvation. Look up Romans 8:15-16 and Galatians 4:6 and make those verses your prayer, asking God to confirm your salvation in your heart. If you are unsure of your salvation, reread this chapter. Believe that what God has testified concerning His Son is true. Remember, God is not a liar. He will do what He has said. If you repent of your sins and put your faith in Jesus Christ, God will not only save you but confirm that salvation in your heart.

3
Christian Certainties—Part 1

Introduction
A. The Certainty of Christianity
B. The Conclusion of the Apostle
   1. His message
      a) Unmask the unreal
      b) Reward the real
   2. His motive
      a) Absolute joy
      b) Absence of sin
      c) Assurance of eternal life
   3. His mandate
      a) Certainty as seen in John's epistle
      b) Certainty as seen in the Old Testament
      c) Certainty as seen in the New Testament
Lesson
I. The Certainty of Eternal Life (v. 13)
  A. The Definition of Eternal Life
    1. According to 1 John 5:20
    2. According to John 17:3
       a) We share Christ's nature
         (1) Our limitation
         (2) Our longing
       b) We share Christ's experiences
         (1) Peace
         (2) Love
         (3) Joy
       c) We possess Christ's fullness
         (1) John 16:15, 23-24
         (2) Ephesians 3:19-20
  B. The Dimensions of Eternal Life
  C. The Duration of Eternal Life
II. The Certainty of Answered Prayer (vv. 14-17)
  A. Identified (vv. 14-15)
    1. The commitment of the Father
    2. The conditions for answered prayer

        a) Confession

        b) Obedience

        c) Submission

B. Illustrated (v. 16)

  1. The historical context of 1 John 5:16

  2. The possible interpretations of 1 John 5:16

        a) It refers to a non-Christian

           (1) The position

           (2) The problems

        b) It refers to a Christian

           (1) The position

           (2) The problems

C. Indicated (v. 17)

  1. Sins of passion

  2. Sins of premeditation

        a) Leviticus 10:7

        b) Numbers 16:1-50

        c) Acts 5:1-11

        d) 1 Corinthians 11:27-32

        e) 1 Corinthians 5:1-8

Introduction

We live in a world of uncertainty and doubt. Everyone struggles with uncertainty. When you buy a car, there is some uncertainty about whether it will run well, so you request a guarantee. When making a purchase we often ask, "Does it have a warranty?" There is the uncertainty of life and health; as a result, much money is spent on insurance. We are purchasing protection against something that has not happened yet. There is the uncertainty of employment, so we have unemployment insurance. Even the government provides some insurance for us in an uncertain world.

A. The Certainty of Christianity

One of the great truths of Christianity is that it is certain. The world doesn't have certainties, but Christianity has absolute certainty.

One interesting Bible study is to take a concordance and look up the words *sure, surely,* and *surety* to find out what is actually sure; then look up *certain, certainly,* and *certainty.* You will find some fascinating things. For example:

1. Numbers 32:23—"Be sure your sin will find you out." That is a certainty.

2. Psalm 19:7—"The testimony of the Lord is sure, making wise the simple."

3. Proverbs 11:18—"To him that soweth righteousness shall be a sure reward."

4. Job 34:12—"Surely God will not do wickedly."

5. Isaiah 53:4—"Surely he hath borne our griefs, and carried our sorrows."

6. Isaiah 55:3—"Incline your ear, and come unto me; hear, and your soul shall live, and I will make an everlasting covenant with you, even the sure mercies of David." This passage is speaking about the sure mercies of God.

7. John 6:69—"We believe and are sure that thou art that Christ, the Son of the living God." The deity of Christ is sure.

8. John 16:30—"Now are we sure that thou [Christ] knowest all things."

9. John 17:8—Jesus said, "I have given unto them [the disciples] the words which thou gavest me; and they have received them, and have known surely that I came out from thee."

10. Romans 2:2—"We are sure that the judgment of God is according to truth." You can be sure God will judge righteously.

11. Romans 4:16—"It is of faith, that it might be by grace, to the end the promise might be sure to all the seed." The promise of salvation is sure.

12. 2 Timothy 2:19—"The foundation of God standeth sure."

13. Hebrews 6:19—"Which hope we have as an anchor of the soul, both sure and steadfast." Christ is that sure anchor in the soul of man.

14. 2 Peter 1:19—"We have also a more sure word of prophecy." Scripture is that more sure word.

15. Revelation 22:20—Jesus said, "Surely, I come quickly."

These are just some of the things Christians can be sure of. They are a sampling of what is said in Scripture to be a certainty. Christians deal in absolute certainties.

B. The Conclusion of the Apostle

John ends the formal argument of his letter in 1 John 5:12 and gives his concluding remarks in verses 13-21.

1. His message

    John's concluding remarks are unlike Paul's customary farewell in that John does not use personal amenities or greetings. His conclusion is a powerful climax to everything he has stated in the epistle. John has given certain tests to identify false teachers, antichrists, and deceivers. His purpose is twofold: to unmask the unreal and to reward the real.

    a) Unmask the unreal

        One result of testing the faith of those who claim Christ is finding out who isn't really a believer.

    b) Reward the real

        The true believers who pass the test can say, "I'm for real." The same test that reveals the unreal gives confidence to the real Christians, which is exactly what John wants them to have.

2. His motive

    John stated his purpose in writing this epistle on three separate occasions.

    a) Absolute joy

        First John 1:4 says, "These things write we unto you, that your joy may be full."

    b) Absence of sin

        First John 2:1 says, "These things write I unto you, that ye sin not."

    c) Assurance of eternal life

        First John 5:13 says, "These things have I written unto you that believe on the name of the Son of God, that ye may know that ye have eternal life."

3. His mandate

    First John is a book of certainties. John writes that if you obey God, you can have certainty.

    a) Certainty as seen in John's epistle

        We see the English word *know* thirty-nine times in this epistle and seven times in 1 John 5:13-21. These

44

references show that Christians have a great deal of certainty. Life isn't a guessing game. God wants us to be certain of some things. In a world where people do not know anything for sure, the certainties in the Bible are revolutionary.

b) Certainty as seen in the Old Testament

(1) Job 19:25-26—"I know that my redeemer liveth, and that he shall stand at the latter day upon the earth; and though after my skin worms destroy this body, yet in my flesh shall I see God." The resurrection of our bodies is a certainty.

(2) Job 42:1-2—"Job answered the Lord, and said, I know that thou canst do every thing, and that no thought can be withheld from thee." Christians can be absolutely certain that God knows all things.

(3) Psalm 20:6—David said, "Now know I that the Lord saveth his anointed."

(4) Psalm 56:9—David also said, "When I cry unto thee, then shall mine enemies turn back: this I know; for God is for me." God is on the believer's side.

(5) Psalm 119:75—The psalmist said, "I know, O Lord, that thy judgments are right, and that thou in faithfulness hast afflicted me." If a person suffers in doing what is right, that is good; and if he is chastised by God, it is deserved.

(6) Psalm 135:5—The psalmist said, "I know that the Lord is great, and that our Lord is above all gods."

(7) Psalm 140:12-13—David said, "I know that the Lord will maintain the cause of the afflicted, and the right of the poor. Surely, the righteous shall give thanks unto thy name; the upright shall dwell in thy presence." It is certain that God will save His people.

(8) Ecclesiastes 3:14—Solomon said, "I know that, whatsoever God doeth, it shall be forever; nothing can be put to it, nor any thing taken from it; and God doeth it, that men should fear before him."

    c) Certainty as seen in the New Testament

        (1) Romans 7:18—Paul said, "I know that in me (that is, in my flesh) dwelleth no good thing."

        (2) 2 Timothy 1:12—Paul here said, "I know whom I have believed and am persuaded that he is able to keep that which I have committed unto him against that day."

First John 5:13 says, "These things have I written unto you that believe on the name of the Son of God, that ye may know [Gk., *oida*] that ye have eternal life." John has given certain tests to unmask the unbeliever but also to give certainty to those who know the truth. *Oida* is used six times in 1 John 5:13-19. It refers to a positive, absolute, knowledge. It is a guarantee outside the realm of human experience, and those who are true believers can rejoice in certainty.

Lesson

First John 5:13-17 gives five certainties of the Christian life.

I. THE CERTAINTY OF ETERNAL LIFE (v. 13)

"These things have I written unto you that believe on the name of the Son of God, that ye may know that ye have eternal life, and that ye may believe on the name of the Son of God."

God wants us to know we have eternal life. Some have said you cannot really know for sure about eternal life, but the Bible says you can. The best available manuscripts do not include the rest of verse 13, so the verse probably ends after the word "life." The phrase translated "that ye may know" is in the present tense and refers to the moment you believe. The moment you believe, you have eternal life. The Christians whom John wrote to may have been unsettled by false teachers and were perhaps doubting their own salvation. But John writes his epistle to assure his readers that if they follow the pattern he prescribes, they will know they have eternal life.

A. The Definition of Eternal Life

Many have wondered what eternal life is. When I was little, I thought eternal life was doing in heaven forever what we do on earth. But eternal life is not simply a definition of time. People in hell will live forever. Eternal life is much different.

1. According to 1 John 5:20

   First John 5:20 says, "We know that the Son of God is come, and hath given us an understanding, that we may know him that is true; and we are in him that is true, even in his Son Jesus Christ. This is the true God, and eternal life." This verse says eternal life and Jesus Christ are one and the same. Eternal life is not a period of time; it is a Person.

2. According to John 17:3

   In John 17:3 Jesus says, "This is life eternal, that they might know thee, the only true God, and Jesus Christ, whom thou hast sent." Eternal life means to know God and Christ. It is not just a period of time but a kind of existence. It is a relationship with God whereby His nature is imparted to us. It is not just a quantity of life but a quality of life. It is having God's life and nature in us. That is what Peter meant when he said we are "partakers of the divine nature" (2 Pet. 1:4). Eternal life is not something we are waiting for; eternal life is the life of God in the soul of man. If Christ is in us and we are in Him, then we have His kind of life right now. The minute God takes up residence in your life—the moment you receive Christ—eternal life begins. Eternal life is sharing the life of Christ.

   a) We share Christ's nature

      Ephesians 2:4-5 says, "God, who is rich in mercy, for his great love with which he loved us, even when we were dead in sins, hath made us alive together with Christ." He takes up residence in us—our life is His life! We think His thoughts, act as He acts, love as He loves, and hate what He hates.

      (1) Our limitation

         Someone might say, "But if I now have the nature of God in me, how come I've still got problems?" The answer is that the life of God in you is limited by your flesh. But some day your flesh will be gone. You will leave your body in the grave when you die and never have to agonize over it again. The day you meet Jesus with your new body, you will be like Him.

      (2) Our longing

         For the Christian, the biggest change that happened in his life was receiving Christ. Death is simply something that occurs along the way. Death is less important than the new birth. The Christian is born into the family of God, and some day with your glorified body you will be like Jesus Christ. Christ is in you now, but someday you will be fully like Him.

b) We share Christ's experiences

    (1) Peace

God is a God of peace, and He wants the Christian to experience peace. In John 14:27 Jesus says, "Peace I leave with you, my peace I give unto you; not as the world giveth, give I unto you. Let not your heart be troubled, neither let it be afraid." Likewise Paul says in Philippians 4:7, "The peace of God, which passeth all understanding, shall keep your hearts and minds through Christ Jesus." Sometimes life might not seem too peaceful to you, but our flesh limits the expression of God's peace in the Christian life. When the flesh is dealt with, then the Christian can experience the true peace of God.

    (2) Love

In John 15:10 Jesus says, "If ye keep my commandments, ye shall abide in my love." The Christian has God's peace and love. Some Christians have trouble loving others. The reason is that the flesh limits love. Only as you starve the flesh can you love with God's love. That kind of love is the same quality and character as God's own love because He has given it to you. John 3:16 says, "For God so loved the world, that he gave his only begotten Son, that whosoever believeth in him should not perish, but have everlasting life."

    (3) Joy

Jesus says in John 15:11, "These things have I spoken unto you, that my joy might remain in you, and that your joy might be full." Whenever you experience joy to its fullest extent, you are experiencing the same joy God experiences. Hebrews 12:2 says we're to be "looking unto Jesus, the author and finisher of our faith, who for the joy that was set before him endured the cross."

Whenever you experience joy to the fullest, you are experiencing the same joy that Jesus experienced when He went to the cross. The flesh will be the only thing that limits total joy in the Christian life.

c) We possess Christ's fullness

(1) John 16:15, 23-24

In John 16:15 Jesus says, "All things that the Father hath are mine; therefore said I, that he shall take of mine, and shall show it unto you." The Father gave all things to Christ, He gave them to the Spirit, and the Spirit gave them to us. Verses 23-24 say, "Whatever ye shall ask the Father in my name, he will give it you. Hitherto have ye asked nothing in my name; ask, and ye shall receive, that your joy may be full." Christians cannot have too high of an opinion of who they are in Christ.

(2) Ephesians 3:19-20

As Christians, we possess the divine nature. That is why Paul prays in Ephesians 3:19 that we "might be filled with all the fullness of God." Paul was saying that all Christians possess that fullness and simply need to appropriate it into their daily lives. Paul went on to say that he prayed that God's fullness would enable Christians to do "exceedingly abundantly above all that we ask or think" (v. 20). Not too many Christians experience this because we limit the fullness of God by the flesh.

The Christian can be certain that he has eternal life. It is the life of God in the soul of man and is not limited by anything but our flesh.

B. The Dimensions of Eternal Life (see chap. 4, pp. 55-56)

C. The Duration of Eternal Life (see chap. 4, pp. 56-58)

II. THE CERTAINTY OF ANSWERED PRAYER (vv. 14-17)

A. Identified (vv. 14-15)

"This is the confidence that we have in him, that, if we ask any thing according to his will, he heareth us; and if we know that he hear us, whatever we ask, we know that we have the petitions that we desired of him."

These verses give us a guarantee of answered prayer. The Greek word for "confidence" is *parrhesia*, which literally means "boldness." We have the true freedom of speech: we can ask God anything according to His will. We can go to God and say, "God, I want to talk to You. Here is what I have in mind . . ."

1. The commitment of the Father

    God is always listening to our prayers. Sometimes my children will say, "Dad," and I am not really paying attention. That isn't like God. In fact, God is more anxious to hear you than you are to talk to Him. God is always waiting for you. You do not force your way into His presence or beg Him for His attention; He has been waiting for you to arrive. If we know God hears us, we know He answers us.

2. The conditions for answered prayer

    Some people pray but do not know beyond that whether God will answer their prayer. God may not answer your prayer when you expect it or how you expect it. God may choose to answer no. But John does give us some conditions for answered prayer:

    a) Confession

    The apostle John wrote, "Beloved, if our heart condemn us not, then have we confidence toward God. And whatever we ask, we receive of him, because we keep his commandments, and do those things that are pleasing in his sight" (1 John 3:21-22). If you are in sin, you are not doing those things that are pleasing in His sight. Psalm 66:18 says, "If I regard iniquity in my heart, the Lord will not hear me." There must be a cleansing of the heart, where sin is confessed and repented of. First Peter 3:7 says that even your family relationships will be hindered if there is unconfessed sin: "In like manner, ye husbands, dwell with them according to knowledge, giving honor unto the wife, as unto the weaker vessel, and as being heirs together of the grace of life, that your prayers be not hindered." We must confess our sins.

    b) Obedience

    John 15:7 says, "If ye abide in me, and my words abide in you, ye shall ask what ye will, and it shall be done unto you." The implication of this passage is obedience.

c) Submission

The primary condition to answered prayer is that it must be made according to the will of God. First John 5:14 says, "This is the confidence that we have in him, that, if we ask any thing according to his will, he heareth us." God will hear our prayers and answer them if they are not against His will. In John 14:13 and 16:23, Jesus says we will receive anything we ask in His name. That is the same as praying according to His will. It is being consistent with His nature. However, James said people do not receive their prayer requests when they ask with wrong motives (James 4:3).

True prayer is asking for something because you know it is what Jesus would want. When you pray according to His will, He answers. Some might say, "What's the use of praying if He's going to do only what is consistent with His own will anyway?" The answer is, He has commanded us to pray. Ours is not to question why; ours is to obey. God is going to fulfill His will, and He wants you to pray so that you can recognize His will, and He wants you to pray so that you can recognize His will as it is fulfilled. If we just ignored Him, we would not know what He was doing in our lives. But as our prayers are aligned with what He is doing, then we will be able to see what He is doing and respond to it.

Praying according to God's will is simply praying for what we know He would want. Try praying this the next time: "Father, I ask this because I know it is what Jesus would want." Sometimes you could not say that and be honest with God. Sometimes your only prayer can be, "Do what You will for Your glory." That is a check system for prayer. God uses our prayers to teach us how to line up with His will. Prayer is the thermometer of your spiritual life. The truth is clear: God grants requests for that which is in His will.

B. Illustrated (v. 16)

"If any man see his brother sin a sin which is not unto death, he shall ask, and he shall give him life for them that sin not unto death. There is a sin unto death; I do not say that he shall pray for it."

John gives an illustration of how God answers only those prayers that are consistent with His will. This particular portion of Scripture is very hard to understand.

1. The historical context of 1 John 5:16

    Whatever the sin that tended toward death was, John obviously knew what it was and so did his readers, because he didn't explain it. That is the difficulty we have and the reason that we have to work so hard to understand the passage. If I had been alive in that day I would have just repeated the passage and everyone would have understood it. But so many years separate the history and language from our understanding.

2. The possible interpretations of 1 John 5:16

    A natural question arises: What does John mean by saying there is a sin that tends toward death? Does that mean a believer can sin and die? Or does it refer to an unbeliever who commits the sin of apostasy? Those are the two prominent views.

    a) It refers to a non-Christian

        (1) The position

             Some say the illustration refers to the non-Christian who pretends to be a believer. This view assumes that life and death mentioned in verse 16 refer to spiritual life and death. It sees the term "brother" referring to a non-Christian. This is a difficult view to take because it uses the term *brother* superficially, not genuinely. It says in effect, "If someone is sinning a sin that does not necessarily result in spiritual death, pray for him and God will give him spiritual life. But, if he has committed the sin unto death, don't pray for him." Those who take this view say that the sin unto death is apostasy—that is, hearing the whole truth of God, rejecting it, and walking away from the faith in defiance of God. As Hebrews 10:26 says, such a one has sinned willfully after receiving the knowledge of the truth. Is John saying to pray for the man who claims to be a brother, because if he is not a total apostate, God may grant him spiritual life? Are we not to bother praying for someone who appears to be an apostate?

Those who take this view also see the man in James 5:19-20 as a non-Christian. That passage reads, "Brethren, if any of you do err from the truth, and one convert him, let him know that he who converteth the sinner from the error of his way shall save a soul from death, and shall hide a multitude of sins." They say this is a non-Christian in the assembly of God who is converted and is therefore saved from spiritual death. That would parallel what John is saying concerning praying for people who haven't committed the sin of apostasy. But if they have committed the sin of apostasy, then those who hold this view say we're not to pray for him because he is out of God's saving will.

(2) The problems

There are several problems with this view, the first being the use of the word "brother." John never calls an unbeliever a brother. The entire scheme of 1 John has to do with those who are the children of God. The second problem is that those who say this passage refers to an unbeliever say he has committed a sin causing spiritual death. But if a person is a nonbeliever, he is already spiritually dead. There is no need to say he committed a sin causing spiritual death because he is spiritually dead already.

b) It refers to a Christian

(1) The position

The other predominant view is that this passage speaks of a true believer. It sees the life referred to in verse 16 as physical life, not spiritual life, meaning God will spare the person's physical life. In other words, if a Christian sins a certain kind of sin, God could remove him from the earth. Verse 16 says, "There is a sin unto death; I do not say that he shall pray for it." John is saying it will not do any good to pray because he is hopelessly lost. If a Christian prays for his sinning brother, God will answer and spare his life.

God will discipline him but won't take his life. If, however, he has committed a certain kind of sin that leads to physical death, it is too late and it does not do any good to pray for him. God will remove him and get him out of the way.

(2) The problems

There are also problems with this view. The context of the whole epistle concerns Christians and apostates, so it seems to fit the overall context to take the first view. But both views are taught in Scripture: Hebrews 6:4-6 and Matthew 12:22-32 teach that a man can apostatize and be beyond salvation. Acts 5:1-11 and 1 Corinthians 11:27-32 teach that a Christian can sin to the place where God takes his life. Exactly which one John is illustrating here is very difficult to know.

C. Indicated (v. 17)

"All unrighteousness is sin, and there is a sin not unto death."

John adds this because even though God forgives sin, that does not mean sin is acceptable. The word *unrighteousness* literally means "lawlessness," which is rebellion against God. Even though God forgives sin, it is still violating His law. Verse 17 ends by saying, "There is a sin not unto death." Compare that with verse 16: "There is a sin unto death." What kind of sin would bring death? There are two kinds of sin in the Bible:

1. Sins of passion

There is the sin that is against the will but occurs in a moment of weakness. It is associated with strong temptation but is not premeditated: it is not plotted out or deliberately planned. It is illustrated in Romans 7, where Paul says, "The good that I would, I do not; but the evil which I would not, that I do" (v. 19). When someone commits that kind of sin, he is grieved, so he repents and turns from it.

2. Sins of premeditation

The second kind of sin is deliberate and premeditated. It is possible for Christians to commit that kind of sin. This is where you sit down and plan in detail. Every time you do it and get away with it, it gets easier and easier. You avoided the consequences once, maybe twice, even three or four times, and it becomes a pattern. This is the kind of sin that tends toward death. It is the prolonged and continued defiant, premeditated sinfulness that brings about the ultimate discipline—physical death.

a) Leviticus 10:7

There are cases of discipline in the Bible where God's people died as a result of premeditated sin. They were not disciplined with the consequence of death for sins of lust or impulsive stealing. Leviticus 10:1-5 records the story of Nadab and Abihu, two sons of Aaron. They plotted a sin in disobedience to God's law by offering a strange fire on the altar. Their sin was flagrant and planned out, and they died because of it.

b) Numbers 16:1-50

Korah and his friends decided to declare themselves priests. They planned to steal the glory that was reserved only for God. The end result was that the ground opened and swallowed them up.

c) Acts 5:1-11

Ananias and Sapphira sold a piece of land they had and pretended to give all the money to the apostles, when in actuality they gave only part of the money away. Peter knew that Ananias and Sapphira had lied and confronted them with it. God killed them where they stood.

d) 1 Corinthians 11:27-32

There were Christians in Corinth coming to the Lord's Table who were worshiping idols and demons, and taking part in the notorious sex orgies. Many of them became sick and some of them even died because they engaged in willful hypocrisy against God.

All sins that resulted in instant physical death were flagrant and premeditated. They all involved hypocrisy toward God because they most directly violated His majesty and glory, which He cannot share with another.

e) 1 Corinthians 5:1-8

There was a man in Corinth having an affair with his stepmother. Paul admonished the Corinthian church saying, "Ye are puffed up, and have not rather mourned, that he hath done this deed might be taken away from among you" (v. 2). Paul then said when that man was taken out of the church, his body would be dissipated in the world, but his soul would be saved (v. 5). God was not going to give the ultimate discipline of death—He put the man out of the church instead. God could have killed him instantly where everyone could see, but God deals differently with momentary sin of passion than with the flagrant, hypocritical sin that endeavors to steal the majesty of God. Premeditated sins lead to death. It is useless to pray for those who continue to sin willfully.

First John 5:16-17 illustrates that God will answer prayer in some situations but not in others. The criterion for prayer is God's will, and it is His will that, at times, causes believers to die because of their continual, premeditated sin. John says not to bother praying for such people. He does not command you not to pray. He says simply, "I do not say that he shall pray for it." God answers prayer within His will. In that we can have absolute certainty.

Focusing on the Facts

1. What is one of the great truths of Christianity (see p. 36)?
2. Christians deal in _____ _____ (see p. 37).
3. What is the purpose in John's message (see p. 38)?
4. State the progression in John's motive for writing his epistle (see p. 38).
5. John writes that if you _____God, you can have certainty (see p. 38).
6. Of the ten verses quoted on pages 39 and 40, name five certainties that Christians can be confident of.
7. What is the meaning of the word *know* in 1 John 5:13-19 (see p. 40)?
8. What is the first great certainty of the Christian life (1 John 5:13; see p. 40)?
9. What does 1 John 5:20 tell us about eternal life (see p. 41)?
10. What does John 17:3 tell us about eternal life (see p. 41)?
11. What limits us from being like Jesus Christ (see p. 41)?

12. What three things can you potentially experience as Christ Himself experiences (see pp. 42-43)?
13. What is the second great certainty of the Christian life (1 John 5:14-17; see p. 43)?
14. Explain what the word *confidence* means in 1 John 5:14 (see p. 44).
15. What are the three conditions for answered prayer (see pp. 44-45)?
16. What does praying according to God's will mean (see p. 45)?
17. What are the two possible interpretations of 1 John 5:16 (see pp. 46-48)?
18. What are the main problems with those views (see pp. 47-48)?
19. What are the two categories of sin in the Bible (see pp. 48-49)?
20. The criterion for prayer is _____ (see p. 50).

Pondering the Principles

1. As pages 36-37 have indicated, the Bible reveals great certainties concerning the Christian life. Take a concordance and look up the usage of one of the following words: *sure, surely, surety, certain,* or *certainly.* Find out what the Scriptures say about what you can be sure of. After you have looked up those passages, thank the Lord for all He has made certain in your life. In a world of great uncertainty, this is a revolutionary assurance of victory. Take these truths and share them with someone you know is not a Christian. Ask God to soften his heart to see truth.

2. John makes clear his reasons for writing his first epistle: He wants believers to experience absolute joy (1 John 1:4), the absence of unconfessed sin (1 John 2:1), and the assurance of eternal life (1 John 5:13). Do those qualities characterize your life? Are you experiencing the joy of the Lord? Do you regularly confess your sins to God? Do you have absolute assurance that you have eternal life? If you have answered no to any of those questions, reread pages 38-43 and ask God to help you work on those areas in your life and begin to make them a daily reality.

3. Many have said you cannot really know for sure about eternal life—but the Bible says you can know for sure. Eternal life is seen not just in terms of the *quantity* of time but in the *quality* of life as well. Eternal life is knowing Jesus Christ. It is sharing His nature and experiencing His fullness. If you have not thought about eternal life in this way before, take time to thank God for giving you eternal life the moment you received Christ. Ask God to help you appreciate your eternal life in terms of its quality.

4. Many Christians struggle with the area of unanswered prayer in their lives. This lesson mentions three conditions for answered prayer: confession of sin, obedience to the commands of Christ, and submission to the will of God. Take each one, and for the next three days do a self-evaluation of your prayer life. As you concentrate on those areas, begin to make a list of answers you receive to your prayers. Contrast the list with your past prayer life, and see if there is a difference in your answers to prayer.

4
Christian Certainties—Part 2

Introduction

Review
I. The Certainty of Eternal Life (v. 13)
   A. The Definition of Eternal Life

Lesson
   B. The Dimensions of Eternal Life
      1. Eternal life begins immediately
      2. Eternal life is a gift
      3. Eternal life must be received
   C. The Duration of Eternal Life
      1. Salvation is not recalled
      2. Salvation is not repeatable
II. The Certainty of Answered Prayer (vv. 14-17)
   A. Identified (vv. 14-15)
   B. Illustrated (v. 16)
   C. Indicated (v. 17)
III. The Certainty of Victory over Sin and Satan (v. 18)
   A. The Plight of the Non-Christian
      1. Dominated by sin
      2. Defiant in sin
      3. Diseased with sin
      4. Damned by sin
   B. The Power of the Christian
      1. Liberated from sin
      2. Living for righteousness
      3. Loosed from Satan
      4. Led by the sovereign God
         a) The Christian's responsibility
         b) The Savior's reassurance
IV. The Certainty of Belonging to God (v. 19)
   A. The Distinction
   B. The Description
   C. The Danger
V. The Certainty That Christ Is God (vv. 20-21)

A. Declaring the Truth
B. Defining the Terms
   1. "Is come"
   2. "True"
   3. "Know"
C. Denying the Traditions

Introduction

One of the great attributes of faith is assurance. Faith is trusting in something you believe is true. The more you believe something to be true, the easier it is to trust it. In 2 Timothy 1:12 the apostle Paul says, "I know whom I have believed and am persuaded that he is able to keep that which I have committed unto him against that day." That kind of belief gave Paul the strength to put his life on the line. Paul also said, "Whether we live, we live unto the Lord; and whether we die, we die unto the Lord; whether we live, therefore, or die, we are the Lord's" (Rom. 14:8). That took away the fear of death. Christianity bases itself on a confident faith. This faith issues itself into a strong commitment to the principles of the Christian life.

Assurance is an essential ingredient of the Christian faith. It is like confidence in that it provides relief from worry. Assurance gives the Christian a joyful sense of liberation. People can face the shadow of death and realize that they have nothing to fear. Assurance is liberation from the bondage of fear and worry. It may express itself in different ways, but assurance gives us the confidence that what God says, He will do.

Review

As we saw in our last study, our assurance as Christians rests upon the Word of God. In 1 John 5:13-21, John presents five great certainties at the end of his epistle.

I. THE CERTAINTY OF ETERNAL LIFE (v. 13; see pp. 40-43)

   A. The Definition of Eternal Life (see pp. 40-43)

     "These things have I written unto you that believe on the name of the Son of God, that ye may know that ye have eternal life, and that ye may believe on the name of the Son of God."

     The first statement John makes in this passage is that we can know we have eternal life. One of the purposes for this epistle was to emphasize that fact. There is no reason to go through life wondering whether you have eternal life. You can know for certain without doubting. If you pass the tests John has given—confessing your sin, confessing Jesus as God, and living a life of obedience and love—you prove you are saved and have eternal life. The primary issue of salvation is eternal life.

Lesson

B. The Dimensions of Eternal Life

1. Eternal life begins immediately

There is much discussion in the New Testament about eternal life. Christians have been accused of living a pie-in-the-sky existence that is unrelated to the present. But eternal life is not something in the future only but in the present. You received eternal life the moment you received Jesus Christ. First John 5:20 says Christ is the true God. The moment you received Christ, you received eternal life.

a) Matthew 19:16—A rich young ruler asked Jesus, "What good thing shall I do, that I may have eternal life?" The issue is a quality of living, where God's very life is imparted to men such as this rich young ruler.

b) Mark 10:30—Jesus promised eternal life for anyone who left everything to follow Him: "He shall receive an hundredfold now in this time . . . and in the age to come eternal life."

c) John 3:15—Jesus told Nicodemus, "Whosoever believeth in him [the Son of Man] should not perish, but have eternal life."

d) John 5:24—Jesus said, "He that heareth my word, and believeth on him that sent me, hath everlasting life, and shall not come into judgment, but is passed from death unto life."

2. Eternal life is a gift

Jesus said eternal life is a gift. But it is given only to those who qualify for it. How do we qualify?

a) John 6:27—Jesus said, "Labor not for the food which perisheth, but for that food which endureth unto everlasting life, which the Son of man shall give unto you." That is the labor of turning from sin to God. Do not labor for a passing fancy but for eternal life. Jesus does not want you to try to earn your salvation but to repent from your sins and turn toward God.

b) John 10:28—Jesus said, "I give unto them [believers] eternal life; and they shall never perish."

c) Romans 6:23—The apostle Paul said, "The wages of sin is death, but the gift of God is eternal life."

d) 1 John 2:25—The apostle John said, "This is the promise that he hath promised us, even eternal life."

e) 1 John 5:11—The apostle John said, "This is the record, that God hath given to us eternal life, and this life is in his Son."

3. Eternal life must be received

The promise of eternal life is seen throughout the New Testament. The Lord saves those who hope for a new kind of living.

a) Acts 13:48—"When the Gentiles heard this [the gospel], they were glad, and glorified the word of the Lord; and as many as were ordained to eternal life believed." The end result for the believer is eternal life. But to receive eternal life, one must receive the salvation offered by God.

b) 1 Timothy 6:12—"Lay hold on eternal life." Paul said the same thing in verse 19. The gift of eternal life is available, but you must make the effort to receive that gift.

Eternal life is at the heart of the gift of salvation. It is God's life in the soul of a man. It is partaking of the divine nature (2 Pet. 1:4), and it occurs at salvation.

C. The Duration of Eternal Life

1. Salvation is not recalled

Eternal life does not just refer to the present; it is also forever. It is not just divine life but eternal divine life. Once God comes into you, He will stay forever. The eternal life that God gives remains within the believer forever. This is why it is called eternal life, not just divine life.

a) John 5:24—Jesus said, "Verily, verily, I say unto you, that heareth my word, and believeth on him that sent me, hath everlasting life, and shall not come into judgment, but is passed from death unto life." God does not take back eternal life.

b) Romans 8:1—Paul said, "There is, therefore, now no condemnation to them who are in Christ Jesus." In Romans 8:38-39 Paul says, "I am persuaded that neither death, nor life, nor angels, nor principalities, nor powers, nor things present, nor things to come, nor height, nor depth, nor any other creation, shall be able to separate us from the love of God, which is in Christ Jesus, our Lord."

c) Hebrews 5:9—The author of Hebrews said, "Being made perfect, he [Christ] became the author of eternal salvation unto all them that obey him."

2. Salvation is not repeatable

a) John 3:14-15—Jesus said, "As Moses lifted up the serpent in the wilderness, even so must the Son of man be lifted up, that whosoever believeth in him should not perish, but have eternal life." It took one look at the serpent in Numbers 21:5-20 for someone to be healed. Likewise, it takes only one look at the cross for someone to be saved.

b) John 4:13-14—Jesus said to the woman at the well, "Whosoever drinketh of this water shall thirst again; but whosoever drinketh of the water that I shall give him shall never thirst, but the water that I shall give him shall be in him a well of water springing up into everlasting life." You drink of the water of life once and never have to thirst again. Salvation is never presented in Scripture as repeatable.

c) John 6:27—Jesus said, "Labor not for the food which perishes, but for that food which endureth unto everlasting life, which the Son of man shall give unto you." Do you know of any food you can eat once and never have to eat anything again? You have to eat the Bread of Life—receive Jesus Christ—only once to live forever.

d) John 6:51—Jesus said, "I am the living bread that came down from heaven; if any man eat of this bread, he shall live forever." You eat this Bread only once.

e) Genesis 2:16-17—"The Lord God commanded the man, saying, Of every tree of the garden thou mayest freely eat; but of the tree of the knowledge of good and evil, thou shalt not eat of it; for in the day that thou eatest thereof thou shalt surely die." If you ate from that tree only once, the consequence was death. Likewise, if you eat of the Bread of Life only once, you will never hunger again. Salvation is always presented as an eternal commodity, a divine, eternal gift. True salvation results in a new kind of divine life that produces righteousness. But even when we sin, there is always forgiveness available. There is no basis for the forfeiture of eternal life.

II. THE CERTAINTY OF ANSWERED PRAYER (vv. 14-17; see pp. 43-50)

"And this is the confidence that we have in him, that, if we ask any thing according to his will, he heareth us; and if we know that he hear us, whatever we ask, we know that we have the petitions that we desired of him."

A. Identified (vv. 14-15; see pp. 43-45)

Prayer: The Christian's Invisible Means of Support

1. John 16:23—The disciples were troubled that Jesus said He was leaving. The Lord calmed them by saying, "In that day ye shall ask me nothing. Verily, verily, I say unto you, whatever ye shall ask the Father in my name, he will give it you."

2. John 11:42—Jesus was praying at the tomb of Lazarus and said to the Father, "I knew that thou hearest me always." Jesus had complete confidence that God always hears and answers prayer.

3. Hebrews 5:7—This was said of Jesus at the time of His crucifixion: "In the days of his flesh, when he had offered up prayers and supplications with strong crying and tears unto him that was able to save him from death, and was heard." Christ was heard in the Garden.

4. John 16:23-24, 26-27—Christ said to His disciples, "In that day [when Christ returns] ye shall ask me nothing. Verily, verily, I say unto you, Whatever ye shall ask the Father in my name, he will give it you. Hitherto have ye asked nothing in my name; ask, and ye shall receive, that your joy may be

full. . . . At that day ye shall ask in my name, and I say not unto you, that I will pray the Father for you; for the Father himself loveth you, because ye have loved me, and have believed that I came out from God." We have the confidence that God hears us because He loves us, and we love the Son. Prayer is the Christian's invisible means of support.

B. Illustrated (v. 16; see pp. 45-48)

"If any man see his brother sin a sin which is not unto death, he shall ask, and he shall give him life for them that sin not unto death. There is a sin unto death; I do not say that he shall pray for it. All unrighteousness is sin, and there is a sin not unto death."

John said there are two kinds of sin. The first type leads to death; the other does not. If you pray for someone who has not committed the sin that leads to death, God will spare his life. His illustration shows that you must pray according to God's will. But if a man has committed the sin unto death, he has brought judgment upon himself, and it will not do any good to pray for him because God has willed to take away his physical life. The other illustration of verses 16-17 is that you can pray for a certain situation and God will act because it is His will. You can pray for the first kind of situation, and God will not act because that is not according to His will. You can pray for the other, and He will act. The apostle John is illustrating the truth that God hears and answers prayer when it is according to His will.

C. Indicated (v. 17; see pp. 48-50)

III. THE CERTAINTY OF VICTORY OVER SIN AND SATAN (v. 18)

"We know that whosoever is born of God sinneth not, but he that is begotten of God keepeth himself, and that wicked one toucheth him not."

A. The Plight of the Non-Christian

1. Dominated by sin

   The natural man is constantly under the power of sin.

   a) Jeremiah 17:9—The Lord said to Jeremiah, "The heart is deceitful above all things, and desperately wicked; who can know it?"

   b) Psalm 51:5—David said, "In sin did my mother conceive me. Man, from the very start of life, is a sinner.

c) Genesis 6:5—"God saw that the wickedness of man was great in the earth, and that every imagination of the thoughts of his heart was only evil continually."

d) Galatians 3:22—The apostle Paul said, "The Scripture hath concluded all under sin." Man is totally lost in sin.

e) John 8:34—Jesus said, "Whosoever committeth sin is the servant of sin."

f) Romans 6:16—The apostle Paul said, "Know ye not that to whom ye yield yourselves servants to obey, his servants ye are whom ye obey, whether of sin unto death, or of obedience unto righteousness?"

g) 2 Peter 2:14—The apostle Peter described false prophets as "having eyes full of adultery and that cannot cease from sin; beguiling unstable souls; an heart they have exercised with covetous practices; cursed children." Everywhere you look, you will find that man is dominated by sin.

2. Defiant in sin

In reality the unsaved person tramples God's laws in hatred and defiance and is an affront to God. The Hebrew word for sin is *pasha* meaning "rebellion." Jeremiah 44:17 gives one of the best definitions of sin: "We will certainly do whatsoever thing goeth forth out of our own mouth." In context, the defiant children of Israel told God they would worship false gods if they wanted to.

3. Diseased with sin

Sin strikes at God and, if it could, would destroy God. It is God's would-be murderer. The Bible says much about the natural man's being diseased with sin.

a) Isaiah 1:5—Isaiah said this about the nation of Israel: "The whole head is sick." Sin brings a total disease.

b) Titus 1:15—Paul said, "Unto the pure all things are pure, but unto them that are defiled and unbelieving is nothing pure; but even their mind and conscience is defiled." The conscience is the monitor of behavior, and if the monitor is defiled, behavior will be impaired. Nothing can cure the disease of sin but the blood of the Great Physician.

4. Damned by sin

   Sin is irrational. It forfeits God's blessing. It is painful and degrading, marring the image of God in man. Sin is damning and leaves men morally weak. It poisons love and turns beauty into leprosy. It defeats the mind, heart, will, and affections. Sin has made the whole world children of wrath. We are objects of God's wrath. Sin brings men under the slavery of Satan, who dominates the world's system. Satan hates man and seeks only to devour him.

   Puritan writer Thomas Watson said, "Satan is the worst tyrant. The cruelty of a cannibal or Nero is nothing. Other tyrants do but rule the bodies, he over the conscience. Other tyrants have some pity on their slaves. Though they work in the galley they give them meat, let them have hours for rest. But Satan is a merciless tyrant, he lets them have no rest. What pains did Judas take, the devil would let him have not rest till he had betrayed Christ and afterwards bathed his hands in his own blood."

B. The Power of the Christian

   1. Liberated from sin

      The world is dominated by Satan and sin, but one born of God has broken the bands of slavery. He is liberated from sin. First John 3:4-10 explains the difference between the believer and unbeliever. Verse 9 says, "Whosoever is born of God doth not [habitually] commit sin; for his seed remaineth in him, and he cannot sin, because he is born of God." One of the things that occurs at salvation is that sin's power over us is broken. The shackles of slavery are severed. The Christian does not continue in a life of sin.

What About a Believer in Sin?

When a Christian sins even to the point that the Lord disciplines him by taking him out of the world, that does not compare to the habitual sin of an unbeliever. People ask me, "What is the difference between a carnal Christian who keeps on sinning until the Lord takes his life and an unsaved person?" The difference is this: The unbeliever does nothing but sin; the believer—even if his sin becomes continual—has his sin-streak broken by deeds of righteousness that evidence his new nature. Christians have broken the shackles of sin. Even when a Christian sins enough to forfeit his life, as Ananias and Sapphira did (Acts 5:1-11), he goes to heaven. That does not give a Christian license to sin habitually—he cannot, because of his new nature—but sin limits his effectiveness, and God takes him out of the world. It is like raising children. Sometimes I feel as if I'm spanking my kids all the time. I think, *Why don't they ever learn?* But then they get to a certain age, and you remember you haven't spanked them for quite a while. As children get older, the frequency of discipline decreases. But every once in a while, they get into a pattern and need to be disciplined. So it is with believers. Sin is not a continuous pattern, but when it surfaces, discipline will result. Nevertheless, Christians are not like the unrighteous, because unredeemed people know nothing but sin. The Christian should not have any patterns of sin at all in his life. And where there is sin, it could even lead to the discipline of death, but the sin of a believer will never match the sin of an unbeliever.

2. Living for righteousness

   Romans 6:15-22 gives us good insight into how sin's power is broken. Verses 15-18 say, "What then? Shall we sin, because we are not under the law, but under grace? God forbid. Know ye not that to whom ye yield yourselves servants to obey, his servants ye are whom ye obey, whether of sin unto death, or of obedience unto righteousness? But God be thanked, that whereas ye were the servants of sin, ye have obeyed from the heart that form of doctrine which was delivered you. Being, then, made free from sin, ye became the servants of righteousness."

   As a Christian, you are freed from the slavery of sin and have become a slave to righteousness. Verses 20-22 say, "When ye were the servants of sin, ye were free from righteousness. What fruit had ye then in those things of which ye are now ashamed? For the end of those things is death. But now being made free from sin, and become servants to God, ye have your fruit unto holiness, and the end everlasting life." The shackles of sin were broken and with it Satan's power over our lives.

3. Loosed from Satan

   The last part of verse 18 says, "That wicked one toucheth him not." Some have asked, "Does this mean a Christian can't even be touched by Satan?" The Greek word for "touch" is *haptetai*, meaning "to fasten on to" or "hold on to." Satan may tempt you, but he cannot possess you because you belong to God. It gives us confidence to know the shackles of Satan are broken. Romans 16:20

makes a great statement about Satan's downfall: "The God of peace shall bruise Satan under your feet shortly." Satan is not over you; he is under you and subject to you.

I have been asked, "Do you believe a Christian can be demon possessed or possessed by the devil?" I don't like the word *possessed* because it speaks of ownership. I believe that demons and Satan can influence you and tempt you, but they cannot possess you because you belong to God. Others say, "How can I continue to live a righteous life and avoid Satan?" Once you become a believer, Satan can never again lay hold of you. Satan cannot fasten onto you (Gk., *haptetai*) or claim you again.

4. Led by the sovereign God

Verse 18 also says, "He that is begotten of God keepeth him." Some Bible translations say the last word of this phrase should be the word *himself*, but the Greek word is *auton* ("him"), not *eauton* ("himself"). The verse should read, "He that is begotten of God keepeth *him*," not, "He that is begotten of God keepeth *himself*." The latter sounds like Christians could keep themselves, which is not true.

a) The Christian's responsibility

There are however some things that Christians are to guard, or keep, themselves. For example:

(1) 1 Timothy 5:22—"Keep thyself pure."

(2) 1 Timothy 6:14—"Keep this commandment without spot."

(3) 2 Timothy 4:7—"I have kept the faith."

(4) James 1:27—"Keep [yourself] unspotted from the world."

(5) 1 John 2:5—"Whosoever keepeth his word, in him verily is the love of God perfected."

(6) 1 John 5:21—"Keep yourselves from idols."

(7) Jude 21—"Keep yourselves in the love of God."

(8) 2 Timothy 1:14—"That good thing which was committed unto thee [the gospel] keep by the Holy Spirit, who dwelleth in us."

There are some things Christians are to keep. But keeping ourselves saved is not one of them. If we had to guarantee our own salvation, that would cause problems, because sometimes we are unaware of what is going on in the spiritual world.

b) The Savior's reassurance

John also says in verse 18, "He that is begotten of God keepeth himself." Jesus Christ is the One begotten of God. It is He who keeps the Christian. Satan cannot touch the Christian, and the reason the believer never falls back into the patterns of total unrighteousness is that he is kept by the Lord Jesus Christ Himself.

(1) Luke 22:31-32—The Lord said to Peter, "Behold, Satan hath desired to have you, that he may sift you as wheat; but I have prayed for thee, that thy faith fail not. And when thou art converted, strengthen thy brethren." Satan wanted Peter, but Jesus prayed for him. Satan wants any Christian he can get. But because Jesus prayed for Peter, Satan gave up. However, he has not given up trying to destroy Christians today. But he cannot destroy Christians, because Christ prays for us, too (John 17:20). If Jesus prays for you, you will be safe in Him.

(2) John 17:12—Jesus said to the Father regarding the disciples, "While I was with them in the world, I kept them in thy name; those that thou gavest me I have kept, and none of them is lost." Jesus did not lose any whom the Father gave Him. The rest of His prayer explains that He is coming to heaven and together with the Father in heaven, the exalted Christ is keeping His disciples. We are kept by our Christ Himself.

(3) 2 Thessalonians 3:3—Paul said, "The Lord is faithful, who shall establish you, and keep you from evil." Satan would like to take you away, but God will guard you.

(4) 2 Timothy 1:12—Paul said, "I know whom I have believed and am persuaded that he is able to keep that which I have committed unto him against that day [when Christ appears]."

(5) Jude 24—Jude said, "Now unto him that is able to keep you from falling." There is no question of Christ's ability to keep us from stumbling. He is able and willing to help us.

(6) Jude 1—The epistle of Jude begins, "Jude, the servant of Jesus Christ, and brother of James, to them that are sanctified by God, the Father, and preserved in Jesus Christ." You are preserved in Jesus Christ. The Lord is in the business of keeping us. Preservation is guaranteed for the overcomer (1 John 5:4-5). The question might be asked, "What about sin?" Sin could result in death but will never change a believer's position once he has received Christ.

Is Salvation Forever?

Robert Gromacki in his book *Salvation Is Forever* gives a good illustration of the difference between the believer's position and his practice of everyday living [Chicago: Moody, 1973, pp. 105-7]. He uses the example of the deliverance of Israel from Egypt (Ex. 4:27—14:31). God told Pharaoh to let His people go, but Pharaoh refused. The result was plague after plague, ending with death to the firstborn of Egypt.

Finally, the children of Israel got out of Egyptian bondage and began to march to the Promised Land. Immediately they began to complain to God and Moses. But when the Lord opened up the Red Sea, they went through, and the Egyptian army, which was pursuing them from behind, was destroyed.

They came to Marah and murmured against Moses because the water was bitter; so God made it sweet. They came to the aptly named Wilderness of Sin and murmured again against Moses and Aaron because of the shortage of food; so God gave them manna. They came to Rephidim and got angry at Moses and tested God because they had no water to drink. So God miraculously produced water out of a rock. At Sinai while Moses was on the mountain receiving the word of the Lord, the people in the valley were breaking the law by making the golden calf. But God spared judgment on the nation because of the prayers of Moses.

Numbers 11 says they marched toward Kadesh-barnea but were tired of the manna God provided. So God sent quail to satisfy their appetites. But their overindulgence brought about a plague from God because they refused to trust Him. The people even voted not to enter the Promised Land. Because of their unbelief,

God chastised them with forty years of wandering in the wilderness.

Later, a terrible rebellion by Korah resulted in the ground's swallowing up him and his companions (Numbers 16). Many tragedies befell the people of God, including shortages of food and a false prophet, who was prepared to curse them if they came into the Promised Land.

You can see from that account that God is gracious. He gave them water when they griped and quail when they didn't like the manna. But God says through Balaam in Numbers 23:19-21, "God is not a man, that he should lie; neither the son of man, that he should repent. Hath he said, and shall he not do it? Or hath he spoken, and shall he not make it good? Behold, I have received commandment to bless: and he hath blessed; and I cannot reverse it. He hath not beheld iniquity in Jacob, neither hath he seen perverseness in Israel." Baalam was saying, "I kept trying to curse them, but the only thing that came out was blessing!"

God said He would bless His people no matter what. He chastised them in the wilderness, and many died. Yet all the time God continued to unfold His blessings upon them, because when God establishes a covenant relationship, it is forever. The occasional sin of His people does not violate it because God sees them positionally in His covenant. And when He looks at you, although you may sin, He sees you complete in Christ. No matter what you do, you cannot violate God's covenant.

The Lord is on guard on your behalf. That is true because the Word of God says it is, because the power of God is able to keep you, and because Christ prayed toward that end. God chose us, and since He wants us, He will keep us. We are kept because we are one with Christ and one in Christ. Because of the nature of redemption, we are kept. The Lord did not die on the cross to lose people but to win them. The apostle John nails down the certainty of eternal salvation.

We know we have eternal life, the promise of answered prayer, and victory over sin and Satan. Those victories are permanent.

IV. THE CERTAINTY OF BELONGING TO GOD (v. 19)

"We know that we are of God, and the whole world lieth in wickedness."

A. The Distinction

Christians are different from the world. This verse gives a very personal touch: we are of God, who is the source of our life and being. In contrast, however, the world lies in the lap of the wicked one. The Greek word translated "wickedness" is the same term used in verse 18, where it is translated "the wicked one." It should be translated "wicked one" in both places because it refers to Satan. The whole world lies in the power of Satan, but Christians are different because they belong to God. That is certain.

B. The Description

The phrase *lieth in wickedness* has several possible meanings. It is used as in a baby being cradled to sleep in someone's lap, a stranded ship lying embedded in the sand, and an animal stuck in a swamp. It could be likened to Samson lying bewitched in Delilah's lap (Judg. 16:19). That is an intimate use of the term. It means that the world actually lies in the lap of Satan. He is personally active in the affairs of unbelievers, but believers belong to God. When man fell, he fell out of the embrace of God into the embrace of the devil. The world listens very carefully to its seducer, comforter, and guide. Satan is the world's pastor.

C. The Danger

There is nothing in or about the system of man that does not lie in the lap of Satan. As Christians, we need to be sensitive to the risk of contamination, because whatever the world touches, it pollutes. The world lies in Satan's lap with its morality, ethics, economics, education, politics, and religion. Everyone belongs to someone. Christians belong to God; the world belongs to Satan. The distinction needs to be clear. It is certain that Christians belong to God, which means we have no part in the world's evil system.

V. THE CERTAINTY THAT CHRIST IS GOD (vv. 20-21)

"And we know that the Son of God is come, and hath given us an understanding, that we may know him that is true; and we are in him that is true, even in his Son Jesus Christ. This is the true God, and eternal life. Little children, keep yourselves from idols. Amen."

A. Declaring the Truth

The certainty that Christ is God is the summation of John's entire epistle. That is the greatest certainty of all. When people question the deity of Jesus Christ, they must not have read 1 John 5:20. The phrase reads, "In his Son Jesus Christ. This is the true God." The incarnation of Christ guarantees every other great certainty we have covered. The Son of God has come to give us an understanding that God is truth and that Christ Himself is the true God. Our faith is not an intellectual theory but an abiding reality based on the deity of the Lord Jesus Christ.

B. Defining the Terms

1. "Is come"

   The term "is come" in verse 20 is in the present tense and therefore means "to come and be present." God has come to this earth and is continuing to give us an understanding of Himself. As a result of faith, we are in God and His Son, who is the true God.

2. "True"

   The Greek word translated "true" is *alēthinos*, which means "real" or "genuine." It is in contrast to verse 21: "Little children, keep yourselves from idols." Since we are in the true One, we are to keep ourselves from false gods and false religions. God is the ultimate reality, as opposed to idols.

3. "Know"

   The Greek word translated "know" in verse 20 is *ginōskō*, which refers to knowing by experience. It is in the present tense, which indicates we are now knowing Him who is true. We are in a constant state of knowing God because we know Christ, and Christ is God. You cannot know God without the Son, and you cannot be in God without being in the Son, because He is God. In essence John says in verse 21, "Little children, stay away from the errors of the heretics, because you are of the truth."

C. Denying the Traditions

Heresy was a danger in Ephesus. For example, the Ephesians were heavily involved in idol worship (cf. Acts 19:23-41). The god of Ephesus was called Artemis or Diana. The Temple of Diana was approximately 420 feet by 250 feet. Hundreds of people lived off the temple trade: priests, eunuchs, temple wardens, and prostitutes. There were many silversmiths who made little idols to sell to pilgrims who came to town. It was not uncommon for a person to buy a silver idol and place it on his chariot. John was writing this letter to everyone who had such idols on their property and was warning them not to worship false gods. The best way they could do that was by believing in and worshiping the true God.

We are certain we have eternal life, answered prayer, and victory over sin and Satan; we know we belong to God, and we know that Christ is the true God. John ends his epistle by saying all that can be said: "Amen"—let it be so.

Focusing on the Facts

1. One of the great _____of faith is _____(see p. 54).
2. Assurance is an essential ingredient of the Christian faith. What does our assurance rest on (see p. 54)?
3. The apostle John has given several tests in his epistle that prove whether or not someone is truly saved. What are these tests (see p. 55)?
4. When does eternal life become a reality in someone's life (see p. 55)?
5. According to John 6:27, there was a labor involved in salvation. What was it (see pp. 55-56)?
6. Eternal life is at the _____of the gift of salvation (see p. 56).
7. When the Lord comes to live in you, how long does He stay? Support your answer with Scripture (see p. 56).
8. What does true salvation produce in the life of a believer (see p. 58)?
9. What is the Christian's invisible means of support (see pp. 58-59)?
10. What does 1 John 5:16-17 illustrate (see p. 59)?
11. What is the plight of the natural man (see pp. 59-60)?
12. What is the difference between a believer in sin and an unbeliever in sin (see pp. 61-62)?
13. Can a Christian be demon possessed? Explain your answer (see p. 63).
14. What are some of the things believers are responsible for in the Christian life (see pp. 63-64)?
15. Why did God continue to meet the needs of the children of Israel in the wilderness (see pp. 65-66)?
16. What is the fourth great certainty in the Christian life (1 John 5:19; see p. 66)?
17. What danger does the world pose to Christians (see p. 67)?
18. The certainty that Christ is _____is the _____of John's entire epistle (see p. 67).
19. What was a particular danger for Christians at Ephesus (see p. 68)?

Pondering the Principles

1. Eternal life is always presented in Scripture as both a quantity and a quality of life. Salvation is given to those who put their faith in Jesus Christ. It will never be recalled, nor is it repeatable. That is why it is called eternal life, not just divine life. Thank God for His gift of eternal life. Think of specific things that have changed in your life since you came to Christ. Write them down and praise Him for each one. Ask God to make more changes in your life that will cause you to see the quality and appreciate the quantity of eternal life.

2. The world is dominated by sin and Satan. As Christians, we have the certainty of victory over both. Look at the areas of your life that are under Christ's control and the areas still under the influence of Satan or self. As you continue to grow in your relationship with Christ, write down the areas that you give Christ complete control of. Keep that list with your Bible and begin to search the Scriptures for wisdom and guidance. Start with the following passages: Matthew 4:1-11; 1 Corinthians 10:13; 2 Corinthians 5:17; 10:5; Colossians 3:1-5.

3. The certainty that Christ is God is the summation of John's entire epistle. It is perhaps the greatest certainty for the Christian. Why do you think so many people deny the deity of the Lord Jesus Christ? If someone were to ask you to show them in the Scriptures where it says Jesus Christ is God, could you do it? First John 5:20 would be a good place to start. Commit this verse to memory along with others that clearly reveal the deity of Christ. You may want to include such verses as John 1:1, 14; 6:44-46; 10:30-33; Hebrews 1:8; and 2 Peter 1:1.

Scripture Index

Genesis
2:16-17   58
6:5   60

Exodus
4:27—14:31   65

Leviticus
10:7   49

Numbers
16:1-50   49
23:19   31
23:19-21   66
32:23   36

Deuteronomy
19:15   21

Joshua
22:2-4   8

Judges
16:19   67

1 Kings
18:20-40   20

Job
19:25-26   39
34:12   37
42:1-2   39

Psalm
2:8-9   12
19:7   37
20:6   39
22:14-16   27-28
22:18   28
22:24   28
31:5   24
51:5   59
56:9   39
66:18   44
119:75   39
135:5   39
140:12-13   39

Proverbs
11:18   37

Ecclesiastes
3:14   39

Isaiah
1:5   60
43:9-12   20
44:8-11   20-21
53:2, 7   28
53:4   37
55:3   37

Jeremiah
17:9   59
44:17   60

Matthew
3:11-12   25-26
3:13-16   24-25
3:17   26
12:22-26   28-29
12:28   29
12:31-32, 34   29-30
18:19-20   21
19:16   55
27:54   27

Mark
1:12   28
10:30   55

Luke
1:35   28
4:14, 18-19   28
22:31-32   64
23:41   27

John
1:12   2

1:15	22
1:32	26
3:14-15	57
3:15	55
3:16	42
4:13-14	57
5:24	55, 57
5:32, 36	22
5:37	19
6:27	55-57
6:51	57
6:69	37
8:13-18	22
8:18	19
8:31	5
8:34	60
10:28	56
11:42	58
12:22-32	48
14:6	24
14:13	45
14:17	24
14:27	42
15:10	42
15:17	44-45
15:26	19
16:15	43
16:23	45, 58
16:23-24, 26-27	58-59
16:30	37
16:33	3
17:3	41
17:8	37
17:12	64
19:30	28
20:31	19

Acts

1:8	32
2:2	37
4:16	37
5:1-11	48-49, 61
10:38	28
13:48	56
19:23-41	68

Romans

6:15-22	62-63
6:16	60
6:17-18	8
6:23	56
7:18	40
7:19	48
8:1, 38-39	57
8:15-16	30
14:8	54
16:20	62-63

1 Corinthians

5:1-8	50
11:27-32	48-49
15:54-57	4

2 Corinthians

9:7	9
13:1	21

Ephesians

2:4-5	41
3:19-20	43
5:8	2

Philippians

2:8-11	28
2:12	9
4:4	9
4:7	42

Galatians

3:22	60
4:6	31

1 Thessalonians

5:5	2

2 Thessalonians

3:3	64

1 Timothy

5:22	63
6:12, 19	56
6:14	63

2 Timothy

1:12	40, 54, 64

1:14	63	4:18	8
2:19	37	4:21	7
4:7	63	5:1	5-7
		5:1-5	2, 5
Titus		5:2	7
1:2	31	5:2-3	8-9
1:15	60	5:4	2, 4-7, 19
		5:4-5	18-19
Hebrews		5:5	6-7
5:7	58	5:6	19, 23-24, 26
5:9	57	5:6-9	23-30
6:4-6	48	5:6-12	18, 21, 23
6:18	31	5:9	18, 30
6:19	37	5:10	19, 30-31
9:14	27	5:10-12	30-32
10:26	46	5:11	32, 56
11:1-2	21-22	5:11-12	31-32
12:1	21	5:12	38
12:2	42	5:13	38, 40-43,
			54-58
James		5:13-17	40
1:27	63	5:13-21	38, 54
4:3	45	5:14	45
5:19-20	47	5:14-15	43-45, 58-59
		5:14-17	43-50, 58-59
1 Peter		5:16	45-48, 59
1:14	2	5:16-17	50
3:7	44	5:17	48-50
4:8	7	5:18	59-67
5:8	6	5:19	66-67
		5:20	32, 41, 67-68
2 Peter		5:20-21	67-69
1:4	41, 56	5:21	63, 68
1:19	12, 37	**Jude**	
2:14	60	1	65
		21	63
1 John		24	63
1:4	38	**Revelation**	
2:1	38	2:7	10
2:5	7, 63	2:10-11	10
2:10-11	7	2:17	11
2:25	56	2:26-28	12
3:4-10	61	3:5	12
3:10	7	3:12	13-14
3:21-22	44		
4:7-8	7		
4:12	7		

3:21	14	16:20	4
6:2	3	21:7	4
12:11	4	22:2	10
13:7	3	22:16	12
15:2	4	22:20	37